ON BEHALF OF
MAUER COSTERISAN
WE HOPE YOU FIND...

... CORAL CASTLE

As fascinating as we do,

Rusty McClure

THE MYSTERY OF ED LEEDSKALNIN
AND HIS AMERICAN STONEHENGE

CORAL CASTLE

RUSTY McCLURE AND JACK HEFFRON

TERNARY PUBLISHING

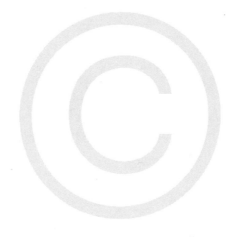

CORAL CASTLE

Library of Congress Control Number: 2009934637

Designed by Stephen Sullivan
Back over illustration of Coral Castle by Tony Greco.
An award-winning illustrator and designer, Tony can be reached at www.tonygrecodesign.com.

TERNARY PUBLISHING

Distributed by The BookMasters Group and Atlas Books

PHOTO CREDITS
Photos throughout the book are used courtesy of the following:
www.123RF.com stock photography: pages xviii, 3, 4
Library of Congress: pages 6, 10-11, 12, 14, 15, 18, 19, 20, 21, 107, 114, 119
First National Bank of South Florida and the Pioneer History Museum: pages 26, 27, 34, 37, 38, 43, 44-45, 49, 59
Coral Castle Inc.: 56, 118
The Levin family collection: 61, 87, 88, 110, 128-129
The Historical Museum of Southern Florida: 54, 67, 78, 84, 90-91, 92
www.somethingweirdvideo.com: 96-97
www.wikicommons.com: 102
Color insert photography by Ian Maguire

To Edward Leedskalnin—
whose vision, intellect, craftsmanship and
courage met head on his severe isolation and loss;
who left to the world a special monument
imbued with imagination, possibility and mystery—
we dedicate this book.

He always called her "Sweet Sixteen"
whenever he mentioned her name,
Someday she would return to him
when his labor of love gained fame!
He would build a show place for her
then she would realize her mistake
She'd leave her simple peasant life
and this Castle a home they'd make.

– Mary N. Yandell,
from her poem "The Mystery of Coral Castle"

TABLE OF
CONTENTS

FOREWORD

I n August of 1992, Hurricane Andrew made landfall just south of Miami, Florida. Andrew was a devastating storm—the third most powerful of the twentieth century—and ended up causing billions of dollars worth of property damage. Hundreds of thousands of people were left temporarily homeless, and dozens of lives were lost in Florida alone.

Of significantly less importance, my family's planned Christmas vacation trip to the Caribbean was ruined. My wife, Amy, and I (and our daughters, aged four and two) decided instead to visit Amy's parents in Miami, Florida. I made sure to pick up a number of pamphlets describing the area's tourist attractions. Most of those attractions fell into two basic categories—animal-themed parks (Parrot Jungle, Monkey Jungle, etc.) and amusement parks (the granddaddy of which, Disneyworld, was just a little too far north for us to make the drive with such young children).

One of those brochures, however, stood out.

It advertised a place called Coral Castle. The castle was constructed of huge blocks of coral rock—oolitic limestone—that had been quarried as single pieces from the ground. Inside the castle were other huge limestone structures—rocking chairs, a sundial, a telescope, an obelisk—quarried from the same material, some of them weighing as much as 57,000 pounds—heavier than the heaviest rocks at Stonehenge, according to the pamphlet. The Castle—built over a half a century earlier—had recently been placed on the National Historic Registry. Odd stuff. Ripley's Believe it or Not Stuff. What was even more incredible...

...the castle was the work of a single man. His picture was in the brochure too. His name was Edward Leedskalnin. He was a Latvian immigrant, a dour-looking fellow who'd come to America in the early twentieth century and spent his life building his forbidding-looking structure.

Not at all the kind of thing two little girls would be interested in seeing. Not at all the kind of thing that I could even take a few hours to see myself, at that point—Andrew had made landfall, as it turned out, in the town of Homestead, where Coral Castle was located, and the entire area (though not the castle itself) was a disaster.

But something about the place—about the little man who'd built it—struck a chord with me.

From time to time over the ensuing years, I would come across mention of the castle. A newspaper article, a radio show, a brief mention in a travel magazine...a lot of people, it turned out, found the story as fascinating as I did. There was, I came to realize, some controversy attached to that story as well. Particularly with regard to Ed's construction methods. You'll read more about that controversy in the pages to follow, but in brief, a lot of people found it impossible to believe that Ed could have accomplished his incredible engineering feats with just the simple tools—the handmade blocks, tackles, pulleys, and winches—readily at his disposal. These people believed that something more was involved. Something almost supernatural—ancient construction secrets, long lost...alien technologies, uncovered...

scientific principles, somehow deduced…these were the things that had made Ed's incredible achievements possible.

A lot of it, frankly, sounded to me like nonsense.

I wasn't a big believer in UFO conspiracies, or that kind of thing—then or now. But I was/am a student of history; it was clear to me that huge technological leaps, when they came along, often turned the miraculous into the mundane.

I had also worked heavy, industrial construction for two summers while I was in college. We poured a lot of concrete in those days—a lot of very, very heavy concrete—and every time I tried to picture Ed working with all that weight, on his own, working with the precision and skill he did…

Something about that picture didn't ring true to me.

I began to wonder. What if Ed really had—as he sometimes claimed—discovered the "secrets of the pyramid builders?" What if there really was something extraordinary in what he had done? That story, true or not, appealed to me probably because it sounded so much like the stories I had been reading since I was a kid. Like Ian Fleming's James Bond novels, every last one of which I had read by the time I finished my junior year of high school. In fact, Ed himself seemed like a character taken from one of those novels to me—the reclusive scientist, whose technological breakthrough made possible…something. What, I wasn't exactly sure of, but in my mind, the more I thought about it, the more I realized this was one helluva story. Or at least the beginnings of one.

But in my mind was where that story stayed.

In the 1990s, when the Internet era came along, Web sites devoted to Coral Castle and its creator began to spring up like dandelions. Each new one offered claims more incredible than the last about what had really happened in Homestead.

Meanwhile, I was hearing some real-life stories of the incredible, from business and military contacts I'd made in the course of my work.

Stories about defense projects, in particular, that seemed the stuff of science fiction themselves. I also began work on a biography of my grandfather and great-uncle—Lewis and Powel Crosley, who had run a series of businesses bearing their name (most famously, the Crosley Broadcasting company) from the 1920s through the 1950s. They had been involved in top-secret defense projects of their own—projects related to their experience in radio broadcasting technology, their expertise in miniaturization of electronic components involving that technology.

At some point, all these ingredients—Crosley Enterprises, the military, Coral Castle, and Edward Leedskalnin—came together in my mind. The beginnings of a story—a plot that would eventually emerge as a novel, *Cincinnatus*—began to take shape. In the course of writing that novel, I finally—fifteen years after Hurricane Andrew touched down—had the chance to visit Coral Castle in person.

I was, frankly, prepared to be disappointed. In my mind, I had built the castle up to such a degree that the real thing, I worried, would be a let-down. A tacky tourist trap. Cheesy, somehow.

As it turned out, I wasn't disillusioned in the least.

Coral Castle was everything that I had dreamed of it being, and more. More than the scattered pieces of information I'd been able to glean from the Internet, and the articles/pamphlets devoted to it. By the time I finished *Cincinnatus*, I knew there was another book I wanted to write. One that, for the first time, would collect all the facts—and a great deal of the speculation—regarding Coral Castle and its creator in one place.

You now hold that book in your hands.

Believe what you wish, as you read the following pages. But when you finish, go see Edward Leeskalnin's creation in person for yourself.

I believe Coral Castle will not disappoint you either.

- *Rusty McClure, October 2009*

INTRODUCTION

Twenty-five miles south of Miami, on the way to the Florida Keys, sits a most unusual roadside attraction. Amidst a busy commercial district of strip malls, gas stations, and chain restaurants, in the shadow of traffic zooming along U.S. 1, stands a structure more of a piece with Europe's ancient megalithic monuments than the roadside kitsch of Southern Florida. A veritable fortress of sculpted stone that occupies a uniquely gray area on the American cultural landscape. Even in the middle of the day, stripped bare beneath the heat of the Florida sun, the place possesses an eeriness that creeps across every jagged surface of the pocked coral stone from which it draws its name. It seems to belong to another world—an ancient, long-lost world, the world of Stonehenge and the ziggurats, the world of Babylon and the mound-builders. It exudes a primitive simplicity, a stunning, natural beauty, a mix of plants and stones, a juxtaposition of organic textures that makes the landscape outside its walls look dull, crass, and phony.

This is Coral Castle.

On Web sites and blogs that champion the existence of UFOs, the lost city of Atlantis, and the magnetic grid theory, it is as significant in human history as the Great Pyramids of Egypt and the Moai heads of Easter Island.

Its creator is significant as well.

He was a European immigrant who came to Florida in 1923 a dying man, diagnosed with a terminal disease, given no more than six months to live. A man who not only managed, miraculously, to survive, but to thrive, to not just live but over the next thirty years achieve one of the most amazing construction feats in all of human history. A man possessed of a dream, and a vision, an odd little hermit, who lived in the woods beyond what was then a remote, sparsely populated town. Driven by that vision, this man pulled gigantic stones from the ground, some weighing as much as thirty tons and some as tall as forty feet, rocks that dwarfed those that had been quarried millennia earlier at Stonehenge. He stood these unimaginably massive stones on end, placing them next to each other so accurately that he needed no mortar or cement in the seams between. With consummate skill he carved the pieces into chairs and tables, into crescent moons and planets. He worked on his masterpiece for nearly thirty years.

Even more amazing—he did this work all by himself, refusing any and all offers of assistance. He used only primitive tools that he fashioned out of old car parts he foraged from a nearby junkyard. And he worked only at night, using the moon and a lantern to light his labors. When nosy neighbors snuck up to find out what he was doing, he somehow sensed their presence and immediately stopped working. Sometimes he called out and let them know that he saw them. Other times he simply slipped away into his living quarters and waited for them to leave.

This man's name was Edward Leedskalnin.

By the time his castle was complete, Leedskalnin—who stood all of five feet tall, who weighed no more than a hundred and twenty five pounds—had quarried 1,110 tons of huge, brittle blocks of oolitic limestone, commonly known as coral rock. He had moved them, carved them, and set them in place with a precision rivaling that of the Great Pyramids of Egypt—whose blocks, weighing only half as much as those he had quarried, were moved by entire nations of the enslaved.

How did he do it?

Back in the day, when people asked, Ed usually would give a sly smile and say that he "knew the secrets of the Great Pyramids." To some, that meant simply he had mastered the art of leverage, that he combined this knowledge with the stonecutting skills learned at his grandfather's knee to create his masterpiece. They would see a large tripod and a number of pulleys on the property and take him at his word.

Others were not so convinced—then or now.

Many believed Ed had mastered (and somehow found a way to break) the laws of gravity. Or that he applied his own understanding of electromagnetic forces (as detailed in the books he would later publish) to create a perpetual-motion generator. Some thought he was able to levitate the rocks he pulled from the ground; others thought he possessed secrets born of alien technology. They find evidence for these beliefs in the mind-boggling shapes, symbols, and formations he placed throughout Coral Castle, which they see as echoing those of ancient Egypt, or the Freemasons, Latvian folklore, or extraterrestrial intelligence.

Standing in the middle of the castle, though, surveying the remarkable achievements all around—the eight-foot stone walls, the twenty-foot table in the shape of Florida, the rocking chairs that weigh literally a ton and still somehow manage to rock—the presence one senses most of all is a human one. Coral Castle speaks first and foremost of the man who built it—of the long, lonely hours Edward Leedskalnin spent yanking gigantic rock from the ground beneath him, of moving, and carving, and shaping that rock. At dusk, on a summer's eve, as the traffic slows, one can almost hear the rasp of his chisel breaking the silence of the dark, humid Florida night.

The work required to build such a place is overwhelming to consider. The story of Coral Castle is indeed a story of magnificent, almost superhuman achievement.

It is also the story of an all-too human obsession.

The story of a man, and a woman, and a broken heart.

A picturesque locale in Latvia in the early 1900s.

1

LIFE IN LATVIA

There has been a lot written about Edward Leedskalnin in the half-century since his death. Magazine articles, newspaper stories, and more recently, Internet sites by the dozens have pages devoted to the man and his creation. Unfortunately, a lot of the information is speculative, undocumented, and sometimes simply wrong. Many errors and unsubstantiated stories have been picked up and passed on, eventually calcifying into "facts" that lack clear sources or any real basis of attribution. Within some fields of study, Ed is legendary, but the legends about him grow more from anecdote and hearsay than from actual research and knowledge.

This is hardly surprising: Ed was, after all, a shy man, a quiet man, a loner who moved around quite a bit. A man who never married, who had no close friends or family in the United States with whom he kept in touch, a man who was not a member of any organizations, and owned no property outside of Florida. He was never part of an immigrant community and didn't leave much behind after his death.

Though he published several booklets about his ideas—from his views on love and politics to electricity and magnetic current—he rarely wrote or talked about himself.

The facts we do have are very slim, particularly when it comes to his early years. And some of those are in dispute. Records of even the simplest things often conflict, such as his birthday (January 12, 1887, according to the registration card Ed himself filled out in 1917; August 10, 1887, according to his death certificate[1]), and his birthplace (a town called Iangubalene, in the Latvian district of Gulbane, according to documents Ed filled out before crossing the Atlantic; Stamayo, according to documents he filed for a border crossing from Canada to the United States in 1913; Stammeina Progasta, according to documents in the Coral Castle Museum; Stameriena, according to other experts).

There is agreement on some of the facts. Ed was the fifth son of Mini (nee Strupkaja) and Andrejs Liedskalnins (a word meaning 'from the mountains'[2]). The Liedskalnins (Latvian words usually place the accent on the first syllable, and the "ns" ending is pronounced with what sounds like an added "h," making the correct Latvian pronunciation of the name *LEED-skul-ninsh*[3]) were farmers living and working in rural Eastern Latvia on rented land. Ed's early years were spent in a lovely pastoral landscape—wide-open fields of rye, oats, wheat, and barley, a hilly countryside where he was exposed to nature in all her glory—but he, and his brothers, were working for much of that time. Working with little hope of a better life for themselves. The boys , like their parents and grandparents, were peasants, trapped by poverty within a rigid class system. A feudal system where the lower classes did not mingle with the upper, where the peasants kept to the fields and the lords to their castles.

As the youngest of five boys, Ed no doubt learned from his brothers, emulating them as they worked the fields and tended the live-

A pastoral scene in rural Latvia, near where Ed Leedskalnin grew up.

stock. Though the work was physically difficult, the peasant farm-ers enjoyed a sense of community. Families remained together and neighbors knew each other well, and sometimes knew each other their entire lives.

The Liedskalnins were most likely Lutheran[4], though it's not known how much they followed the tenets of the church. What they—and their neighbors—were all attentive to, what they all celebrated, was the cycle of seasons, especially the summer solstice. The celebration of the solstice was combined with the feast of John the Baptist to form the national holiday of Midsummer, on June 24. In Latvia the day is called Jāni or Jānis, on which traditional songs are sung, and revelers gorge on cheese and beer. Men wear oak wreaths and women wear wreaths of flowers. Ed retained his sensitivity to, and appreciation of, the cycles of nature throughout his life, which he made clear in some of his sculptures at Coral Castle.

Old castles were a common sight in Latvian when Ed was a boy and
surely inspired the design of his own castle.

Ed did attend school, according to most up to the fourth grade.[5]
It would be wrong, though, to assume that because he received so
little formal schooling he was uneducated. Ed absorbed knowledge
not just from books, but from those around him—his peers, his el-
ders, his family. By the time he was in his twenties, he could read,
write, and probably speak at least three languages.

There was something else he'd become expert at as well by that
point. Something he learned from his father, uncles, and brothers, a
skill that was passed down from generation to generation of Leedskalnins: the art of cutting stone. By the time Ed was an adult he'd
years of experience as a stonemason working on everything from
tombstones to the huge castles belonging to his lords and masters.

It was a skill that was to serve him well later in life.

✦ ✦ ✦ ✦ ✦

In the late nineteenth century, Latvia, as it had been since 1721, was part of the Russian Empire. Political and military power was held by Moscow. Latvians, outside of those in the capital city of Riga, were generally poor farmers and artisans, living as virtual serfs in what remained of a feudal society.

Change, though, was in the air.

A general unrest among the lower classes throughout Europe and the development of socialism sparked a growing nationalistic movement in Latvia. People began to object to the oppressive conditions within the country. They wanted not just a change in the social order, they wanted to run things themselves.[6] Latvians, like most other peoples under the sway of Imperial Russia, objected to the oppressive, autocratic rule of Czar Nicholas II, and the conditions he imposed on them.

By the time Ed was in his late teens, young men of his age burned with the dream of a better life and a country of their own. They swelled the ranks of the Latvian Social Democratic Workers' Party, so much so that by the turn of the century, that party, despite the huge disparity in the size of countries, outnumbered its Russian counterpart. Prominent among those young Latvian men was one of Ed's brothers, Otto, who often spoke at political meetings.[7]

On January 9, 1905, in the streets of St. Petersburg in Russia, a group of demonstrators gathered to deliver a petition to the Czar, a petition that pleaded for the government to show greater leniency in dealing with its workers. Unrest exploded into bloodshed as soldiers fired into the crowd. Hundreds of people were killed and wounded.

A few days later, on January 13, ten thousand strikers gathered in sympathetic support on the banks of the Daugava River in Riga. Soldiers fired on them, killing seventy-three and wounding many more.

Russian Czar Nicholas II

When the gunfire erupted, many people ran onto the ice-covered river and drowned when the ice gave way.[8]

The slaughter sparked a full-scale uprising in Latvia—just as sympathetic strikes and demonstrations throughout the Russian empire ignited other uprisings. In the eastern regions of Latvia, peasant farmers burned the estates of their German lords, and months of violence ensued. Attempts by the military to break the uprising failed. Martial law was declared in August. The czar demanded retribution, arresting thousands, exiling many to Siberia. Ed's brother Ernest was arrested and sent to prison in St. Petersburg.[9]

Evald Liedskalnin, Otto's son, believed his uncle Ed was involved in the revolt as well:

> "My father told me that when the Black Hundred [Russian Cossacks working for the czar] came, Ed left for the Lubana forests to join the partisans. Otto said that Ed always walked about with a rifle hidden underneath his coat. Once he met with a Cossack patrol and just calmly walked on…if he had run, they would have shot him for sure, without asking if he was partisan or not."[10]

Regardless of whether or not Ed was actively involved in the revolt (there is no firm proof of his participation), his life was deeply affected by it. He was an impressionable eighteen-year-old, who had just witnessed the destruction of his country's budding nationalist movement. He had seen the terrible retribution on the demonstrators by both the Russian government and the German aristocracy. People he knew were killed or were exiled to frozen wastelands from which it seemed they might never return. He saw family and neighbors flee, abandoning the land that had been their home for generations. Some fled the country altogether, going to London and other cities in England. Approximately five thousand emigrated to the United States, doubling the Latvian population in America.[11]

By 1912, Ed had decided to emigrate as well. There are some who say that he left because of fear of retribution by the czar's police. Ed's brother Otto told his son Evald that: "...Ed was pursued by the czar's police and could not stay in Latvia any longer."[12]

Others—Latvian writer and editor Andris Straumanis prominent among them—doubt that Ed left for those reasons. By 1912, Straumanis believes, fear of reprisals from the 1905 uprising were long since past.[13]

In years to come, when Ed would talk about why he'd ultimately decided to leave Latvia, he would refer only obliquely to his 'troubles' with the Russians.

More often than not, he would talk about something else—or, rather, someone else.

Her name was Agnes Scuffs.

She was the girl he had been planning to marry.

The two met, according to one of those legends that have grown up around Ed, at some point contemporaneous with the turn of the century's political uprisings. Agnes was ten years Ed's junior. He met and fell in love with her when she was still in her teens, proposing to her shortly thereafter. She accepted. A wedding date was set and a place was chosen, a small church in the town of Veculbene.

And then, for reasons unknown, Agnes changed her mind.

Ed's grand-nephew Janis Leedskalnin told Andro Stavris, author of *Korallu Pils*, exactly what happened at the ceremony, as it had been relayed to him by his grandfather Jakebs and grandmother Lizete, who were among the invited guests.

Agnes and Ed were standing together at the altar. The priest approached, and asked each of them in turn if they were ready to commit to the other. Agnes could not find it in her heart to say "I do." She turned away and left Ed standing at the altar, alone.

After a moment, he hurried after her. And subsequently vanished.

According to Janis, he was never seen again in Latvia.[14]

A tangled web of speculation has grown up around the reasons for Agnes' actions. Some say that her mother forbade the wedding because Ed was too old. Or that he was too poor—a mere peasant would not do for her daughter. Others say that Agnes was in love with another man, perhaps a friend of her father's who lived in England. Still others say that the girl Ed would long for the rest of his life was not Agnes Scuffs at all but instead a young woman named Hermine Lusis.[15]

The disappointment—the embarrassment—were, according to Janis, the primary reasons Ed decided to emigrate.

"It is absolutely clear that Ed left for America because he was jilted by his bride," Janis declared.[16]

Thomas Lorman, professor of Eastern European Studies at the University of Cincinnati, agrees. "[Ed] becomes a laughing stock. A twenty-something to be turned down by a sixteen year old? It's a pretty appalling slap. It's a slap of class distinctions."[17]

That slap may have been the final push in a direction Ed was already contemplating. The political situation in Latvia remained messy, and the drums of war had already begun to beat on the horizon. The wedding gone wrong, then, may have confirmed for him the notion that it was time to try his luck elsewhere.

He may have been thinking he would leave for only a year or two before returning to his homeland, as many immigrants did at the time. If so, he was mistaken.

On March 23, 1912, Edward Leedskalnin, like so many others of his generation, departed Europe for America—the land of opportunity.

He was never to return.

8902. P.Z. - RIGA LE QUAI

The port of Riga, Latvia's capital and largest city.

Immigrants sail into the port of New York, circa 1912.

2

WANDERING AMERICA

On March 23, 1912, Edward Leedskalnin, in the company of two companions, Ernst Warsell[1] and Bertha Schmidt,[2] boarded the ocean liner S.S. *Pennsylvania*, departing out of Hamburg, Germany, bound for New York City. Hamburg was one of Northern Europe's main ports, a primary departure point for the peoples of many European countries for their voyage to America. As Ed waited, the crowd around him chattered in German, Russian, Polish, Hungarian, and other languages, a din of confusion and excitement, sad partings and final farewells. They stood bundled up in heavy coats, the men wearing bowler hats, the women swaddled in shawls, some holding babies, others urging their children to stay close so they didn't get lost in the crowd.

Most photographs we have of Ed were taken in his later years. In these pictures, he appears skinny, even gaunt, wearing a stern look on his face, dressed in a dark suit and tie, his posture as rigid as a post. He looks dour, forbidding, even a little bit scary. Not at all a man one would want to spend time with, much less marry.

The port of Hamburg, Germany, from which Ed embarked
on his voyage to America.

A photo of him from right around the time of his voyage to America, however, reveals an entirely different aspect of Ed's personality. In this picture, Ed is wearing a sporty bowler and tie, a thin moustache, and a look of shrewd confidence. He looks quite the continental character; quite the enterprising young man. And no wonder: at the time, his life was open to new and tremendous possibilities. Life in America would be different for him. Hard work and resourcefulness, rather than the class into which you were born, determined the level of success a person could achieve. Success in business, in one's personal—and one's romantic—life.

No one in America would reject Ed for what—rather than who—he was.

As he left for the New World on that cold March day, he must have been brimming with hope about his future in the new land.

The information on the passenger list gives us our first documented glimpse of Eduard Letzkalin, which is how he spelled his name on the manifest. The information he provided illuminates—and in one case contradicts—basic tenets of the Leedskalnin Legend, as it has developed through the years.

Ed states that he is twenty-five years old.[3] He is able to read and write and is in good health. He writes that he is 5'6" tall—a claim emphatically contradicted by people who knew him later in life.

"We used to call him Mr. Leprechaun because he was so small," stated Florida City resident Charlotte Schmunk.[4]

"He was tiny. I kind of looked down to him a little bit,"[5] said petite Ruth Campbell, a resident of Homestead and the curator at the Historic Homestead Town Hall Museum.

The *S.S. Pennsylvania* carried Ed across the ocean.

"He was a little man," concurred Frances Boysen, another Homestead resident, who once ate Thanksgiving dinner with Ed at the home of a relative.[6]

The height that is listed—either Ed's claim or the estimate of the government clerk, then, seems like an exaggeration, given that Ed's real height, according to his neighbors, was closer to five feet tall.

In filling out the documents required for his passage to America, Ed listed himself as *"Landmann, Tagelohner,"* a landsman who works for daily wages, a day laborer. He listed his nationality as Russian, his race as Lithuanian—not as much of a contradiction as it may seem, because although Lithuania is located south of Latvia in the Baltic region, the areas share much in common culturally, and the languages are very similar. His family, in fact, may have had its roots in the Lithuanian region.

He also stated on the passenger list that he was carrying eighty dollars, considerably more than typical immigrants brought with them, according to genealogist Sharon DeBartolo Carmack. "Most immigrants had around twenty-five dollars on them," she said. "So anything more than that is a lot."[7]

According to the Consumer Price Index, his eighty dollars in 1912 would be equal to a little more than $1,800 today. Not a fortune, by a long shot, but certainly enough to support Ed until he found work in America. Perhaps Ed had been saving his money for the pending nuptials with Agnes, or perhaps his family pooled resources to help him on his way.

Regardless of how much money he had, it is more than likely that Ed, given his station in life and his pecuniary ways, took a berth in third-class steerage. Passengers in steerage usually brought their own food—cured meats, fish, pickles, cheese—and the air would have been redolent with those smells[8] for each hour of the sixteen-day crossing. The ocean in March would have been choppy with storms and winds as well, and many of the passengers would have been seasick, at least for the initial portion of the voyage. The *Pennsylvania*—unlike the new ocean liners being built at the time (such as the White Star Line's *Titanic*, which sank a week after Ed arrived at the Port of New York)—was not built for luxury.

✦ ✦ ✦ ✦ ✦

On April 7, 1912, the ship arrived in New York—at Ellis Island, the gateway to the New World. Ed and his companions Worsell and Schmidt, in the papers they filled out, gave New Brunswick, New Jersey, as their final destination. They were headed, in fact, to Berta Schmidt's home, where Bertha's husband, Robert, who was also Ernst's cousin, awaited them.

Though Latvians had been immigrating to the US for many years—and their numbers swelled with those who arrived in the wake of the 1905 uprising—they never came in large enough numbers to establish a strong presence in any one place. Unlike the Italians and Poles, who created their own neighborhoods in the industrial cities of the East, or the Scandinavians, who settled in the upper Midwest, Latvians never settled in concentrations large enough to provide a place where new arrivals like Ed could settle in and feel at home, could prosper from a network of countrymen who had already established connections in America.[9]

For whatever reason, he didn't stay long in New Jersey. In August of 1912, he crossed the border into Canada. From documentation he would later fill out, we know that during the four months he spent in the U.S. after his arrival, he lived in "various states." Eventually, he decided the grass would be greener, so to speak, in the Pacific Northwest.

"As far as opportunities for manual labor, [it] would have been one of the best places to go," says Robert Ficken, author of *The Forested Land: A History of Lumbering in Western Washington*. "Thousands of

Ed was processed through the famous immigration center at Ellis Island in New York, shown here and on the next page.

people were going there every year. When you got here, getting a job would have been simple."[10]

By this point in the new century, the focus of the lumbering industry had shifted from the upper Midwest to the Pacific Northwest, where huge forests of cedar, fir, pine, and spruce blanketed the region.

Ed started his search for work in Cranbrook, British Columbia, a town in the Canadian Rockies about thirty-five miles from the American border. Cranbrook, an important stop along the Canadian

Loggers in the Northwest, during the time Ed worked there.

Pacific Railway, was the population and transportation center of the mountainous East Kootenay district. He only stayed four months, crossing back into America (at the town of Eastport, Idaho) on January 9, 1913. On papers filled out for that crossing, he listed Spokane, Washington, as his final destination.

He also listed himself as 5'9" tall.

In those days Spokane was a major rail hub and was a key transportation link to the Northwest from all points east. Ed would have arrived there to find chaos similar to the kind he'd witnessed back in Hamburg—a roil of passengers hustling from one platform to the next, the urgent call of porters announcing "All aboard." Only this time, since he spoke little English, the crush of people and sounds and sights around him must have seemed not only strange and exotic but maybe even a little frightening. Ed was all alone, half a world away

Life in the Northwest logging industry during the early twentieth century was often difficult, dirty, and dangerous.

from his home, his family, from even a single familiar, friendly face.

He would spend the next ten years of his life that way.

The next hard evidence we have of Ed's movements comes from his draft registration papers, filled out on June 5, 1917. By that time, he was living in Douglas County, Oregon, in the small town of Elkton. Required by law to register for the First National Draft,[11] Ed claimed exemption because he was the subject of a foreign country. He still had not applied for citizenship, and one wonders if he planned to return to Latvia sometime in the future. A few months before Ed went to register for the draft, the czar had been deposed in the Russian Revolution. One wonders if Ed still harbored feelings about an independent Latvia and if he was, perhaps, tempted to return.

On the card, Ed declared that he was employed by "himself"

and that his occupation was "Axhandle manufacture." A supplier of tools for the logging industry, rather than a logger or mill worker. Physically, Ed described himself as slender, with blue eyes, and light brown hair.

He also, in response to a question on the form regarding height ("tall, medium, or short—please specify") described himself as of 'medium height.'

By January of 1920, he had left Elkton and moved even farther west, to the coastal town of Reedsport, Oregon, home of the newly founded Reedsport Lumber Company. According to papers he filled out for the 1920 census, Ed lived in rented property there, with a man named Clement Somers. Somers was a native of Oregon and worked in one of the Reedsport lumber mills, as did Ed at this time. But not for too much longer.

"It was a young man's job," says Robert Ficken. "The conditions were rough. You could get badly hurt or killed. It was dangerous work, exacerbated by the employers who were always trying to get as much production as possible from the workers. If you were injured, there was no unemployment insurance, no social security, no welfare. If you put in eight years of hard work in the woods, you'd come out a much older man than your years."[12]

By the early 1920s, Ed was in his thirties and ready to move on. From the logging industry, and from the Northwest as well. The weather was cold and wet much of the time. The work days were ten to twelve hours long, and loggers worked those days in damp clothes, indoors and out. Filth and disease were rampant. At some point, as Ed would later tell his neighbors, he got sick. He decided to go someplace warm, where he could have a fresh start, find an opportunity that held greater promise.

His immediate movements after Reedsport, though, remain somewhat of a mystery.

Some sources say that Ed moved next to California, perhaps for the sunnier climate. Some say that while there, he met a rancher who hired him to drive a herd of his cattle back to Texas.[13] Ed would later tell his Florida neighbors that during these years he bought stock in some utility companies, the dividends from which supplied him with money for the rest of his life.

The truth about Ed's wandering years is difficult—if not impossible—to know for certain.

In 1923 Ed showed up in Florida City, Florida, intending, at last, to put down roots. To build himself a home.

First, however, there was the concern about that illness he'd caught in the logging camps. Which in the intervening years had worsened.

The disease, according to many, was tuberculosis, which in those days often amounted to a death sentence.

It is at this point in Edward Leedskalnin's life that the few facts we do have begin to be colored by myth. The story of his wanderings, and his achievements, begin to move from reality, into the realm of the unbelievable.

Ed stands at Ed's Place, in the late 1920s.

3

BUILDING A CASTLE

I n 1922, the *Miami Herald* was known as the heaviest newspaper in the US due to the number of land listings advertised in it. The twenties were boom years in Florida. From 1920 to 1925 the state's population more than doubled. When whole towns grew up almost overnight and others doubled and tripled in size. Improved roads and a railroad line from New York to Florida brought newcomers seeking pleasure and prosperity by the thousands to the Sunshine State. Miami Beach, Boca Raton, Ft. Lauderdale, West Palm Beach, and countless other towns rose up from the Florida soil to beckon eager vacationers south. Meanwhile, easy credit in the post-war economy attracted land speculators hoping to cash in on the promise of this lush warm-weather wonderland.[1]

One of those was a man named Ruben Moser, who in 1910, along with a number of neighbors and family members, left Topeka, Kansas, for a chance to start afresh in the Sunshine State. Moser settled in the southernmost part of Florida, near a twenty-two-thousand-acre parcel that in 1913 was purchased by the Model Land Company of Detroit.

Florida City, Florida, in the early 1920s.

The company quickly began a marketing effort that extolled the virtues of this tropical paradise to people in Michigan, going so far as to rename the parcel of land Detroit. Some Michiganders took the bait and moved in. Those who did, however, quickly realized that the promotional brochures painted a far more attractive picture of the place than they found. Before long, most moved away. In 1914, portions of that development were incorporated under the name Florida City.[2] Located on the eastern border of what is now Everglades National Park, approximately thirty miles southwest of Miami, it became the southernmost city in the United States not located on an island.

By that time, Ruben Moser had become a real estate agent, as well as one of the area's most vocal ambassadors. An article in the August 6, 1914, *Homestead Enterprise* reported "through [Moser's] untiring efforts and honest zeal the Redland District has become known to hundreds of people who might otherwise have been ignorant of the opportunities here."

Florida City was a small farming community when Ed arrived.

Thanks in part to Moser's efforts, by 1922, Florida City had gained a population of over 800 people. The city, according to the town's official Web site, "had a drug store, a hardware store, and a three-story hotel. South of the town was the largest Ice Plant in the state and a lumber mill; however, most of the town's economy came from farming."[3]

At some point while out driving during the winter of 1922–1923, Moser came across a man lying in a heap alongside the road. He helped him up, put him in the car, and brought him home. The man, Moser and his wife soon discovered, was seriously ill with some kind of respiratory disease. He was on the verge of dying.

That man, of course, was Edward Leedksalnin.

✦ ✦ ✦ ✦ ✦

Ed had, apparently, arrived in Florida in the winter of 1922–1923. The weather was certainly milder than that of the Northwest. The sun must have felt good on his face, a welcome relief from the gray, damp days in Oregon. Instead of tall Douglas firs towering under leaden skies, he saw palm trees and palmettos, fruit trees heavy with oranges and grapefruits, cypress, flowering camellias and bougainvillea.

The Florida City he came to was an area made up mostly of small farms, undeveloped land, palm trees, scrub pine, and swamp. The state's economic boom did not extend as far south as Florida City. If Ed had journeyed to this part of the state looking to get in on the action, he was out of luck.

He may, however, have had other reasons.

No one knows how long Ed traveled before Moser found him. Joe Bullard, the author of a fictional account of Ed's life titled *Waiting for Agnes*, heard a story that suggested Ed had been wandering for months. Bullard has appeared on a number of radio shows to discuss his years of research on Ed and Coral Castle, and after one appearance he was contacted by a man who said Ed had walked a long way to get to Florida City. Bullard recalls the man telling him:

> My father was working in Jacksonville in a bank. He looked outside one day and saw this little guy walking along the road with a witching rod. He said the little guy seemed out of it and might need some help. He asked the little guy what he was doing, and the guy just said, "When I find it, I'll know it." When Ed became famous, my father saw his picture in the paper and said that was the little guy on the road with the rod.[4]

The rod, according to some, was a "witching" or dowsing rod believed capable of determining the presence of water or so-called "energy" within the earth. Local people who knew Ed often mentioned that he was very aware of water tables and talked about them frequently.

This is the first known mention of Ed being guided by what some term "supernatural" forces.

The first public documentation of Ed's arrival in Florida City appeared in the February 27, 1923, edition of the *Homestead Enterprise*, the local newspaper. It offered a short, straightforward statement: "E. Leedskalnin a Californian has purchased an acre of the R.L. Moser homestead and is planning to erect a home soon."

The paper didn't mention the miraculous recovery that Ed had made from the often-fatal disease he had caught.

In her book titled *The Villages of South Dade*, historian Jean Taylor wrote that "One day Ruben Moser brought home Edward Leedskalnin, a ninety-seven-pound Latvian immigrant, who was seriously ill. Mrs. Moser fixed a room in a tool shed for him and nursed him until he recovered."[5]

There are those who believe that statement contains the whole truth of the matter. As one of Ed's neighbors would later recall, "he told me he was unable to work, was why he came here—that he had a Lung Condition, and the Climate cured him and made him so strong, and healthy."[6]

These people believe that after living in the Moser's tool shed for a few weeks, sitting in the sunshine and resting, and enjoying the ministrations of Frances Moser and Lois, the Moser's teenage daughter, Ed started to regain his strength and feel better. Tuberculosis (if that is indeed what Ed was suffering from) is an infectious disease caused by airborne bacteria. Its symptoms usually include chronic coughing, fever, and weight loss. It was not curable in the early 1920s. Significant progress in the treatment of the disease, in fact, was not made until 1946 with the success of the antibiotic streptomycin.[7]

A common treatment for the disease at that time was exposure to ultraviolet rays, gotten from sunlight. Moving to Florida may have been Ed's last-ditch effort to heal himself. He counted on the warm sun of Florida to cure him, and it did.

Others believe the story is not that simple.

According to another neighbor, Ed's disease was far too serious to be cured by simple sunlight. "He went to see Dr. B.F. Eckman who examined him and told him that his health was in such a condition that he could not live more than six months. He told [Ed] to get fresh air and do the things he wanted to."[8]

The doctor, in other words, gave Ed a death sentence.

Three years later that same doctor called on Ed and was (in the neighbor's words) "never so surprised to find the fellow he said could live such a short while."[9]

Sunlight does not qualify as an answer to the riddle of Ed's miracle cure.

How then did he manage to survive—never mind thrive, and find the strength to build his Coral Castle—for nearly thirty more years?

Some theorists suggest that he cured himself through a unique understanding of electromagnetism, which he would later write about in great detail. They suggest this magnet therapy, in combination with the healing effect of the sun's ultraviolet rays, led to Ed's miraculous recovery.

Joe Bullard, among others, believes that Ed's tuberculosis remained a lifelong problem for him and that he continued to use this type of therapy. Bullard suggests Ed lay out in the sun while wrapped in a cable attached to a power generator—to give himself magnetic treatments to continue to fight the disease. The castle today still includes what Ed called his "sun couch," a circular stone on which he lay to take in the warm—and healing—rays.

However he cured himself, by winter's end, Ed had made enough of a recovery to leave the Moser's home. And shortly thereafter, he bought an unlikely parcel of land from Ruben Moser—two acres located in a remote area unsuited for any type of commercial enterprise. Two acres completely unsuited for farming; two acres whose topsoil barely covered a foundation of coral rock that ran hundreds of feet below the surface.

He apparently took a long time to find those two acres. As Jean Taylor wrote: "Leedskalnin searched the whole neighborhood for land which met his requirements."[10]

And what were those requirements?

Edward Leedskalnin wanted to build himself a home.

And the kind of rock that lay underneath Ruben Moser's two acres was perfect for his desires.

In 1955, half a decade after Ed's death, the new owners of the home he had spent his life building hired a woman named Bodil Kosel Lowe as a "publicity agent." Their intent was to document the unbelievable, while such documentation was still possible. To have in hand affidavits—sworn testimony—that would attest to the truth that the 1100 tons of coral that comprised Edward Leedskalnin's home had been quarried, raised, cut and lain in place by him, and him alone.

Lowe spent from April through September of that year gathering those affidavits—from 285 local residents in all—as well as accompanying commentary, after which Lowe, a notary public, affixed her seal.

The documents they signed states:

> That _____ personally knew the late Edward Leedskalnin, and from actual knowledge can attest to the fact that the said Edward Leedskalnin began the construction of Rock Gate at a location in Florida City, Florida, on or about the year 1921, and sub-

sequently moved some of the objects to its present location and continued the work until his death in December 1951; that he cut from the ground, moved and carved the huge weights of coral rock into the art creation known as Rock Gate without the aid of any individual or individuals; that the tools found presently on the premises are the identical and same observed by the affiant on visits to Rock Gate while Edward Leedskalnin was alive, and in the process of constructing Rock Gate; and that the said Edward Leedskalnin was unmarried and lived alone on the premises during the period of the construction of Rock Gate and until his death.[11]

These papers provide the best glimpse of not just Coral Castle's construction but of Ed's early years in Florida City.

From the affidavits:

"In 1925 we saw Ed with his chains and tools working away on his project, a most amazing achievement."
- Mrs. C.L. Greenlands

"This is to certify that I knew Edward Leedskalnin from 1921 until the time of his death. I was often a visitor at the original location and often talked to him as a true friend." - S.L. Shields

"I have known the above—Edward Leedskalnin for thirty years. And have spent many hours of my youth with "Old Ed"—watching him with a hammer and chisel working on solid rock; and I know for a fact that the above statements are true." - L.O. Cloninger, Sr.

"I knew Ed since 1924.... I was his shoemaker and he came often to my shop and I was always very interested in him and his work. I thought it was grand that a little lightweight man could undertake and do what he did and I saw it with my own eyes. He told me he came to Florida as he was sick in the north. And he felt better living here." - David Friedrick.

And on and on they go. Most laud Ed as a gentle, genial man. They shed light on both his personality and his early relationships with his neighbors. They speak of visiting his place on tours, for picnics and church socials, and of seeing him in town or riding his bike.

The affidavits, though, cannot capture the curiosity their signers must have felt upon first seeing the little European man, new to the area, as he began what would be his life's work.

From the start, according to most, he remained elusive. He worked during the night, by moonlight, by lantern. Stories circulated of his keen hearing, his unusual sensitivity. Ed seemed, somehow, to know when he was being watched.

Local resident M.C. Bardsley can still recall the time her mother took the family to the castle site, late in the evening, in hopes of catching a glimpse of Ed at work. "He only worked in the dead of the night and everybody knew that," she said. "And my mother was pretty sneaky. She was trying to prove that we could watch what was happening. Because, to her, that was part of history."

Bardsley, laughing at the memory, adds that the investigation was unsuccessful. "We just sat in the car and watched and nothing happened. About four o'clock mother took us home. We were there about five hours."[12]

An early photo of Ed's Place in Florida City.

Others found the process far less mysterious. While their affidavits agree that Ed did the work himself, there is no mystery to some as to how he did it.

> "During the time I was attending Homestead High School studing [sic] a course in General Science, our instructor took the entire class to Edward Leedskalnin's place in Florida City so that Mr. Leedskalnin could show the class how he cut these huge rocks from the ground and how he (by himself) lifted them out of the ground and stood them in place with the aid of simple block and tackle rigs and long pry poles. The class was studing [sic] weights, and the methods of moving articles with a minimum of effort. This was about 1930."[13] – T.A. Zajim (Assistant Postmaster)

"He showed how he used pine logs to lift rocks. He would tie one end while he placed another wedge, keep this up till he got the piece on wooden rollers and moved where he shaved pieces with a hatchet."[14] – David Freidrich

"As a boy in the 1920s, about 1928 or 1929, I was a neighbor of Edward Leedskalnin, and I saw him dig out and raise the large moon stone and set it up, the map of Florida stone, and several of the rocking chairs. When he was digging out the high slender stone, with a star on top that weighs 18 tons, I well remember he broke the first two stones. It was on his third try he patiently quarried the masterpiece that still stands today.

"In the beginning of his quarrying operation of each stone, he would dig a ditch about 18" wide all around his desired shape. He then would drive lots of wedges all around the stone and break it loose. In prying the stone out of the hole, he would use a small telephone pole. If that wasn't strong enough, he would connect another pole, using steel band straps. If the second pole extension was not sufficient to pry it out, he would attach buckets to the end and fill them with pieces of iron."[15] – Earl S. Lee

In his book *Mr. Can't Is Dead*, Orval Irwin, who may have known Ed better than any of his Florida neighbors, describes the process step by step and even includes diagrams.

Many people believe that Ed was able to build Coral Castle because he was a gifted engineer and stonemason. We know that he was trained as a stonemason in Latvia and possessed a mastery of the craft. We also know that he worked for a number of years in the logging industry in the Northwest, where enormous trees were cut down and then placed on various forms of conveyance before being shipped miles away. It's more than likely that through these years of experience Ed learned the means of moving huge logs.

We also know that Ed had a block and tackle as well as smaller pulleys and hoists, some of which still hang in the workshop on the first floor of the castle's tower. Several photos show Ed using a large tripod made from telephone poles with a block and tackle dangling in the middle that would allow him to lift a cut stone from the ground and pull it upright.

One part of the story is indisputably true: To quarry, carve, and place the huge rocks, Ed used tools fashioned from old car parts taken from a nearby junkyard. Making such tools was an accomplishment in itself. Using them to create stunning formations required a resourcefulness that borders on genius.

To build his castle using these simple tools, he first would have dug down through the thin layer of topsoil and removed it, then used a saw or wedges to cut the brittle oolite rock, creating a trench around the piece he wanted. He then would use long steel wedges to get beneath the rock and pry it up, inserting smaller wedges to keep the stone raised high enough that he could wrap a chain beneath it. Slowly he would begin raising the rock with the pulley, inserting larger and larger wood blocks beneath the rock until it reached the surface, when he would place it on logs that would allow him to roll it where he wanted it to stand. Finally he would use the pulley to slowly raise the stone, inserting wood blocks until the stone stood upright.

It is worth keeping in mind, of course, that the stones Ed supposedly moved in such a manner were as heavy as thirty tons.

The tripod Ed used to help move the huge stones in Florida City.

And yet there are many who doubt the truth of this explanation. They feel that Ed, in describing the process by which he constructed Coral Castle, was deliberately misleading his neighbors, hiding the secrets he possessed, offering explanations that didn't tell the full story. They doubt that Ed's ten-ton hoist was capable of lifting the tallest and heaviest pieces of coral he quarried—and then moving and placing those pieces so precisely.

Ed's Place in the late 1920s. Ed used the wooden shack in the center as his living quarters during the years in Florida City.

Among those doubters are some surprising people.

In April 1958, *Civil Engineering* magazine published a short article titled "Projects of Florida Builder Baffle Engineers." Written by a man named Carroll Lake, the article addresses the question of how Ed managed to achieve such results through standard engineering methods. Given that the magazine targets a readership of engineers, the article offers disappointingly little technical analysis[17] but does offer high praise for Ed's skills, noting "The scarcity of stone chips shows he made no false moves and no mistakes."

Lake's evaluation of the rock gates—the stone entranceways Ed constructed for his castle—is particularly interesting:

"The construction of [these] speaks volumes for the uncanny accuracy of Leedskalnin's engineering knowledge. He had to know the pivot points exactly—without guesswork or trial and error—and to hang the gates in perfect balance. The fact that the gates are of porous coral and uneven in density increased the difficulty of figuring the balance points."

The gates, more than any other aspect of the castle, cast doubt on the theory of Ed's using only engineering skills and simple tools. How could he have balanced those gates so precisely while the chain-wrapped stone was suspended from a block and tackle? He may have been skilled enough to quarry such huge stones with his simple tools, but it's tough to imagine him using those tools to move the rocks into place so exactly that there is barely a seam between them. And then to balance the rocks so that they swing with the slightest touch?

When reading about the size and weight of the stones, it's difficult to believe one man—even a talented engineer—could do it alone. Standing next to them, it's nearly impossible.

Ed sitting on one of his rocking chairs at Ed's Place in Florida City.

4

FLORIDA CITY AND A MONUMENTAL MOVE

We have no records of when Ed completed construction on what he called "Rock Gate," or "Rock Gate Park." Or the year that he first opened his attraction, which would soon come to be known in the area as "Ed's Place," to visitors and tourists.

One of the earliest advertisements for that attraction appeared in the January 3, 1932, edition of the *Miami Daily News*. Under the boldface headline "MR. REAL ESTATE MAN" runs the subhead "LOOK OVER ED'S PLACE AND SEE THE POSSIBILITY OF MAKING MONEY."

The suggestion is he was intent on selling the place, but the text of the ad merely hopes to entice tourists. That text—from a marketing standpoint, not to mention a grammatical one—is so bad that if any tourists made the trip as a result of the ad, their visit would have been as miraculous as the castle itself.

The ad reads as follows:

Go to Ed's place and have a new experience. Bring your camera. You will want your picture taken. More than 17,000 people have seen the Ed's Place [sic]. Make yourself one more, than more than 17,000 [sic].

Come before noon if possible. Home all day Sundays and Holidays. Am usually out from 2 to 4:30 P.M. weekdays. Here are the directions: Go to Florida City, then three-quarters mile west on Palm Avenue to Redland Road, then one-half mile south on Redland Road, then one-quarter mile west to ED'S PLACE. ADMISSION 10¢. Clip this out now so you will have the road directions handy at all times.

The ad is accompanied by two photos. One shows the castle as it stood at that time, with Ed's shack rising above a line of trees behind the wall. The second shows Ed sitting in a rocker next to the Florida table, wearing a white shirt and dark tie. His pose is formal, his posture rigid, his hands placed stiffly on his thighs.

Where Ed came up with the "more than 17,000 people" number is a mystery. He certainly didn't have a turnstile. If he had opened his attraction for visitors in 1924 or 1925, giving him a year or two to fashion enough pieces to begin drawing attention, he would have been in business for six or seven years by the time he wrote this ad. Given that only eight hundred people lived in Florida City, word of his "unusual accomplishment" must have spread pretty quickly—or he may have been exaggerating, as he did with his height on the documentation forms. Whatever the number, people obviously were visiting the attraction—enough, at least, to give him the money to run a large ad in a Miami newspaper. (In 1936, he would publish a small booklet in which he would claim "more than fifteen thousand people...have seen Ed's Place.")[1]

By the late twenties Ed was welcoming visitors to his 'place' on a regular basis. And by then he was beginning to formulate the speech

Lewis Cloninger, one of Ed's many neighbors in Florida City,
visits during the 1930s.

Visits to Ed's Place were a popular Sunday outing.
This one appears to have occurred in the early 1930s.

he would give to those visitors while he gave them a tour of his unusual "home." And at the center of that tour, from the very beginning, was the story about the girl he had left behind in Latvia. The
girl who had left him at the altar. His Sweet Sixteen.

"That's all he ever talked about," says Charlotte Schmunk, who
played at Ed's Place as a child in the 1930s. "He'd tell that story over
and over." She remembers that he often would look off into the distance as he talked about his lost love. "He didn't seem to be of this
world," she says. "His mind was elsewhere."[2]

According to a number of local residents interviewed through
the years, Ed would often look to the sky when speaking of her. As if
picturing her in his mind.

He told visitors that he was building the place to win back her
love, a castle for his queen, who someday would return to him. Yet
there are no records showing if Ed wrote letters or sent photos back
to family and friends in Latvia, or if he ever tried to contact Agnes.[3]

There are those who doubt she really existed.

Some speculate that Ed's lost love sprang entirely from his imagination, that she may, in fact, have been based on secrets feelings he
harbored for Lois Moser, the teenage daughter of Ruben and Frances
Moser, who had nursed Ed back to health when he arrived in Florida
City.[4] Still others believe that Agnes did exist, but by the time he
began building his monument to her—more than ten years after the
broken engagement—he had idealized her into a mythic creation that
had little to do with the real person.

Orval Irwin, who seems to have known Ed on a more personal
level than the other local people of the time, offers his view:

"When anyone visited [Ed], he enthusiastically went through the
story of how and why he built the place for her. He always had so
much enthusiasm that one would have thought that she was going to
arrive at any moment. He talked about her for so many years that

people wondered if she had really existed. I believe she did, because he couldn't have been inspired to design and build his tender love story in stone without her love in his heart.... Personally I doubt the real story of Ed and his 'sweet sixteen' was ever known."[5]

Irwin is clearly right about the depth of Ed's feelings, and the inspiration he drew from them. Whether those feelings were sparked by an actual person or one Ed created in his mind, however, remains an open question.

✦ ✦ ✦ ✦ ✦

Ed's ad also gives us a sense of how he spent his day. We know already that he worked at night; we now learn that he was 'usually out' from two till four-thirty in the afternoon.

Some speculate he used this time to sleep, having worked through the night. Others believe he used it to study. (We question the wisdom of telling everyone in the Greater Miami area when he would be gone, especially given that he was supplying them exact directions to his house.)

Saturday was Ed's day out of the castle, supported by reports from locals who say he spent the day at the Seminole Theater, either watching people from a perch outside, or watching movies inside. Orval Irwin recalls frequently seeing Ed at the theater during the late 1920s, when movies were still silent. When the "talkies" arrived in the early thirties, Ed stopped going, saying that the dialog confused him.

"... on Saturday afternoons, we would find Ed in the parking area out in front of the theater," Irwin writes. "He would be dressed in his best clothes: dark pants, an elaborate white shirt...a dark bow tie, suspenders, a dark hat. He sat on his bicycle seat and wore a friendly smile."[6]

Irwin notes that Ed enjoyed watching people do their Saturday shopping. Though genial when people spoke to him, he mostly would sit and watch. Irwin also recalls that he and other young people in town sometimes would head to Ed's Place "to have a wiener roast." They would call out to Ed and ask him if it was okay that they used his property: "The answer was always, 'It's OK! Come on.' He would come out to the fire and answer our questions about his work. The atmosphere there was always so hospitable that some of us wondered if he wasn't from the 'southern' part of Latvia."[7]

Next to the ad, the paper ran a short article without a byline—apparently an early form of advertorial. The article heaps praise on Ed's creation, though at one point the unnamed author calls it a "caveman's castle." Ed himself is described as "a slender, wiry man, scaling 120 pounds" who claims to have performed all the work on the site himself without assistance from anyone, including "mule, negro or other helper."

As for the castle itself, it was "quarried by hand from pits nearby, using only rock ax, crowbar, sledges and an ingenious arrangement of levers." The phrase "almost incredible" is used to describe Ed's feat. The writer does not speculate as to whether or not any of the massive stones were made or placed by supernatural means.

The article also mentions "a radio aerial" stretched between the top points of two structures Ed had built—the obelisk, and the crescent moon. Ed had built his own radio by that time, the remains of which are on display at Coral Castle. Radio was still a relatively new technology in the late 1920s, but Ed's interest in science—as well as his ingenuity—already was apparent. For those who see deeper meanings in the castle and in Ed's work, claiming that the castle was some type of power station to communicate with UFOs, there's an eerie resonance to the writer's statement that "the owner likes to comment jokingly that he gets his music from the heavens."

By the date of the Miami paper's article/advertistement, Ed had been in Florida City for nearly ten years. He'd made friends with many of the people who lived there. They visited his place, even used it for social gatherings. He had become a familiar sight in town—pedaling his rickety bike, sitting and

Ed spent many Saturday afternoons at the Seminole Theater in downtown Homestead.

observing the shoppers in downtown Homestead outside the Semi-nole Theater. He shopped at Florida City stores for the few supplies he needed, sometimes trading the vegetables he grew for crackers, sardines, bread, and milk.

But behind his friendly smile he remained aloof and distant.

He would take help from no one, not even a ride in a car. Other than his Saturday outing to town and occasional trips for necessities, he stayed in his castle, never going anywhere. Perhaps he continued to pine for his Sweet Sixteen. Perhaps he thought of home and of returning. Or perhaps he focused mostly on his plans for new sculptures in his park or on his experiments with radio and electricity.

By early 1937, he had something else to focus on as well.

Ed had decided it was time to move—and he was taking his massive Rock Gate with him.

And he was going to do it, of course, on his own.

Like almost every aspect of Ed Leedskalnin's story, the rationale behind his move is a subject of debate.

One of the most commonly stated reasons given for Ed's decision to relocate was that he had heard about a plan to build a new housing development near him in Florida City, and he was afraid that the influx of neighbors would ruin his privacy.

This theory seems unlikely. First of all, his place in Florida City was not located in a growing area. In fact, more than seventy years later, it's still relatively undeveloped. Given the Herculean task of moving so many tons of brittle rock, it seems doubtful Ed would have moved simply because he heard a rumor about a residential development. He was not an impulsive man.

"Nothing ever happened, nothing went in there," recalls local historian and long-time resident Ruth Campbell. "There was nothing around. He was out there by himself." Campbell went on to give what she felt a more likely reason for Ed's decision: "He just eventually figured out that it wasn't going to be a tourist attraction down there in Florida City."[8]

In a 1939 newspaper article, Ed gave the same answer—he wanted to locate his attraction where tourists could more easily find it. That summer, the *Redland District News* published a piece about his move, titled "Ed Is Doing a Colossal Job of Moving But He Wants No Help, Thank You." The article, which ran without a byline, noted, "Ed's place has attracted many tourists through the years. But this new place, near the highway, should prove much more convenient for the winter visitors, he believes."[9]

Orval Irwin agreed with this assessment: "Of course we could understand why [he moved], for that was the main road for traffic from Miami to Key West."[10]

The new property—ten acres, as opposed to his original two— was right on U.S. 1, the Dixie Highway, the main road on which tourists traveled while heading to the Everglades and the Keys. Ed may have been a recluse, but he wanted people to see his work—and to pay for the privilege. As roads improved and the Great Depression slowly began to wane, vacationers were beginning to come down the highway in greater numbers. The Florida City-Homestead area was becoming less remote. We know that Ed for a number of years had been buying newspaper advertisements to tempt tourists to visit his attraction. The move was intended to increase his share of that tourist business.

Or not.

Another theory frequently given about why he moved focuses on coral rock, suggesting that Ed had quarried all he could at Florida City. Given the depth of oolitic limestone in that section of Florida, he certainly hadn't used everything on his property. But he might have dug as deeply and as widely as he could with his primitive tools. Or found that he'd used all the rock that was easiest to access and position. Perhaps, people suggest, he had dug as deeply as he could to allow the rocks to be unearthed without breaking.

And there is another reason sometimes given for the move: fear.

The story goes that one night in Florida City, Ed was robbed by a group of young thugs seeking a large sum of money they'd heard was hidden somewhere in the castle. In an article published in 1972 in the *Miami Herald*, William Jinks wrote:

"One day when he'd finished the tours, he noticed several young men loitering about the entrance to his place. Thinking that something might be amiss, he walked over to them.... They wanted the money they'd heard about. Leedskalnin protested that there was no money...and...to prove he was telling the truth, he emptied his pockets, causing a small number of coins to spill on the ground.... One of them grabbed Ed from behind, while another began to hit him. They eventually knocked him out without getting him to change his story. They fled with the few coins and left Ed where he had fallen."[11]

The article features some of the most evocative writing ever published about Ed Leedskalnin, but the writer, unfortunately, offers no sources for his richly dramatic story, details of which do not appear with such specificity in any other publication. He quotes neither written sources nor personal interviews.

Earlier in the article the writer creates a vivid scene in Latvia where Agnes tells Ed she is breaking off the engagement. It occurs, however, more than a year after we know he was living in the United States.

Poetic license appears to have been taken in the latter case; it's quite possible it was taken in the former as well. Nevertheless, the beating has entered Leedskalnin lore.

And then there are those who believe that Ed's decision to move had nothing to do with tourism, or privacy, or coral rock, or the lack thereof.

The decision to head for Homestead in the late 1930s, they say, was the result of an earlier miscalculation on his part, having to do with the earth's energy grid.

This grid—sometimes called the magnetic grid—is made up of a hypothetical network of lines, called ley lines, that crisscross the earth and allegedly connect a number of megalithic places. The concept was created in 1921 by an amateur archaeologist from England named Alfred Watkins, who noticed that a number of these places in England could be connected by straight lines.[12] Believing he had discovered an ancient network of trade routes, Watkins did not attach mystical associations to the lines.

According to the theory, the places where these ley lines intersect hold tremendous electro-magnetic power. Stonehenge in southern England and the Great Pyramids in Giza, among other mysterious places in the world, are located at intersections in the energy grid.

Ed's new property, the ten acres on U.S. 1, was located at an intersection point as well. The westernmost point, in fact, of a particularly well-known geometric structure contained within the grid.

The Bermuda Triangle.

Those who believe that Ed chose his new location for Rock Gate because of its relationship to the energy grid find support for their theory in Joe Bullard's story of the man from Jacksonville, whose father saw Ed on the road with a "witching rod," which can be used not only to find the location of underground water, but to detect points of energy on the grid.

They believe that Ed's move was sparked by a realization on Ed's part that earlier calculations that led him to Florida City were incorrect, and that relocating to Homestead would put him in closer alignment to the grid, allowing him to thereby draw more power from it.

The leading books on the subject are *The Energy Grid*, by Bruce L. Cathie (1997) and *Anti-Gravity and the World Grid*, an anthology of grid-related essays compiled by David Hatcher Childress (1987). Cathie, a former pilot from New Zealand, has become a de facto spokesperson on the subject. His essays are included in the Childress book, and his own book contains an essay on Coral Castle, titled "The Diminutive Man of Mystery." Beyond the rather swashbuckling sobriquet, Cathie bestows upon Ed the power to locate the grid and draw from it. He writes:

"Ed Leedskalnin had not moved on to the Florida site by chance. This geometric position was extremely close to one that would be ideal for setting up harmonics related to gravity and light harmonics. The fact that [he] had access to secret knowledge is much more evident in the relationship of Coral Castle to the world energy grid system."[13]

We will return to Cathie's speculations regarding the energy grid—and their possible relationship to Edward Leedskalnin's almost superhuman feats of engineering—in a later chapter.

A tour guide in the 1950s moves the nine-ton rock gate with one finger. Theorists point to the gate as proof that Ed drew from the energy grid in building his castle.

Ed stands in the courtyard of Rock Gate in Homestead.

5

AT HOME IN
HOMESTEAD

E
d purchased his new property—ten acres of land located in an
area just north of Homestead called Modello—on April 28,
1937. He paid ten dollars for it.[1] The land had come on the
market as a result of the bankruptcy of its owner, J.W. Boone.[2] Ed
found out about the situation and bought the property as soon as it
became available—the very next day, in fact, which suggests he had
been contemplating the move for some time.

Moving from one house to another is a considerable task for anyone, but when you're taking the house with you and it weighs nearly a
thousand tons, the task is considerably more difficult. For the average
person, it would be nearly impossible. But for Edward Leedskalnin—
who had cured himself of a supposedly incurable disease, who rou-
tinely set enormous monolithic rocks on end—it was just another
challenge to overcome.

In his book *Mr. Can't Is Dead*, Orval Irwin recalls talking to Ed
about how huge a job he was undertaking: "When asked, he smiled
and said, 'It'll take a long time, but I'll do it!' Time didn't mean much

to him—it was the objective that really counted."[3]

That, and taking charge of the move himself.

Just as he had done while building the castle, he worked on the move in solitude, mostly at night. The article in the *Redland District News* cited earlier suggests his insistence on working alone was related to the castle's appeal: "He wants to tell them that this is not going to be one of these tourist places where the 'folks get fooled.'"

Others are convinced it had more to do with Ed's desire to conceal his "secrets."

He could not, however, complete the task entirely on his own. He needed a vehicle of some sort to transport the pieces of Rock Gate Park north to Modello, and his bicycle wasn't going to be up to the task.

Orval Irwin's book spends several chapters discussing the move, beginning with his own role in the process. Irwin writes that in 1937, when he was fourteen years old, he had an old flatbed pickup truck, and Ed asked him to help haul some tools to the new property, agreeing to pay him a dollar for each trip.

They made two such journeys, filling Irwin's truck with Ed's primitive, homemade tools, along with his various pulleys and winches. Irwin offers a fascinating description (as well as some drawings) of the process, detailing how Ed secured his tools at the new, empty property.

"… his tool house was a trench about six feet deep, eight feet long, and two feet wide. The pit was protected by a ladder on top, chained down and locked at each end with a padlock. Concrete anchored the bottom of the chains…. The sides of the trench had been hand cut with a neatness that would have you believe it was machine dug. Nearby, all the materials removed from the hole were neatly graded into three piles; sand, small rock, and heavier coarse rock. I took note of this, because it was typical of Ed's work, and part of the secret of his accomplishments— making every lick count and letting nothing go to waste.[4]"

Irwin's truck, however, would not be able to help move the heavy

Krome Avenue in Homestead—the town's main street, where residents
watched as Ed hauled his huge stones to his new property.

stones that comprised the heart of Ed's roadside attraction. Even if
the engine had been strong enough to pull such a load, the tires would
never stand the strain.

Ed determined that what was needed was a vehicle with solid
tires rather than inflated ones. He found what he was looking for in
a tractor owned by a local farmer named Bob Biggers.

The engine was only half the puzzle, however. To actually haul
the coral, Ed fashioned a trailer from the nearby junkyard, using
the chassis of an old Republic truck with boards laid across it. One
by one he loaded the massive stones onto the trailer and then called
Biggers, who would hitch the trailer to his tractor and haul the crazy-
looking collection up the highway. When they arrived, Biggers un-
hitched the trailer. Ed would then unload the multi-ton pieces all by
himself, telling Biggers he would be in touch when he was ready to
have the empty trailer hauled back to Florida City. Irwin states that
Ed took "two or three weeks" to load and unload, but Biggers recalls
it taking less time.

"I'd unhitch the truck and he'd say, like if it was Friday, 'Come back Tuesday and I'll be ready,' and I'd go back Tuesday and sure enough, there it was, all ready. He always knew exactly when he'd be finished."[5]

The mystery of this process is obvious: how did Ed load and unload these pieces all by himself and then place them one by one to create his new castle? Theorists can point to his ability as a stonemason to try to explain his ability to raise the huge stones. But getting them on and off a trailer and then moving them into position?

Irwin's description of Ed's tool shines some light on the subject:

"Of all the articles I hauled that day, the most impressive one was his home-made winch. He had found a pine tree with a six-inch diameter trunk and a long outstretching root growing out from it. He cut this tree about three feet above the top of the trunk, then dug up the stump, along with the root, and mounted it horizontally on a heavy long frame. The stump could then be revolved by the handle, which was the long three foot outstretched root. It was operated by a bolt through a small piece of pipe, both placed through the root end. This pipe turned around on the bolt and served as the handle. The home-made rig gave him a tremendous power to wind cable, using the stump as a winding drum. With this, he pulled those huge rocks on his rollers. It was his most powerful piece of early earth moving equipment."[6]

It's possible Ed had seen this type of equipment—whether home-made or jerry-rigged—used by loggers in the forests of Oregon and Washington to move the giant spruce, fir, and pine trees. It's also possible the winch may have been his own invention, another piece of equipment attesting to his resourcefulness and engineering genius.

If Ed was secretive about how the stones were loaded, he apparently was less concerned about his neighbors seeing the gigantic load slowly rolling up the highway to his new home. Among the 1955 affidavits, a number of people mention seeing the bizarre sight of Bob Biggers driving his tractor along the road, pulling a trailer that con-

Ed worked tirelessly to build the tower
and the walls at his new place.

tained gigantic stone crescents and chairs and the other pieces from Ed's Place. Bob's sister, Mrs. C.U. Barnes, writes: "He moved all of the rock objects alone from Fla. City. He would put them on a big trailer, then have my brother Bob Biggers come and pull them to the present location. Then he would say to Bob to go on now for I don't want any one to bother me while I work."[7]

Mrs. Lula Belle Tisdale writes, "I visited Ed's Place in Florida City and saw it being moved up the highway to its present location."[8]

Georgia Neill Waters writes, "I saw Ed's Place being moved on the highway to this new location."[9]

Others make similar statements, all of which attest that the moving of the stones was not done in Ed's typical surreptitious manner. One affidavit, however, does contradict the others. Mrs. Ruth Tomerlin writes, "My brother-in-law moved the rock constructions for him. He said Edward Leedskalnin loaded the truck at night by himself & the following morning my bro-in-law had the truck moved to the new location where Ed unloaded the truck too."[10]

Her statement contradicts Irwin's, which contends that Ed took several weeks to unload the trailer. It's also at odds with Bob Biggers' description of the process (it's not clear if Biggers was Mrs. Tomerlins's brother in law).

A few other names have been mentioned when locals discuss the move. Frances Boysen recalls that her father-in-law, Casper Williams, helped Ed.[11] Several people may have pitched in along the way, though no one saw the stones being loaded or unloaded, taken down or put back up.

That part of the work, Ed insisted on doing alone—and doing it when no one could watch him.

He began the move in late spring or early summer 1937. He finished it sometime in 1939. He did not sell the Florida City property until he was finished, and he began setting up the stones at his new place even before all of them had been removed from the old.

When the monumental task was finished, near the bottom of the towering obelisk he had constructed and then moved, Ed carved a series of dates into the stone. Sometime in the early 1940s, he dressed up in a dark suit and had a photo of himself taken in front of the obelisk.

In the picture, he is pointing to those dates (which remain visible to this day) with obvious pride. They read as follows:

MADE 1928

MOVED 1939

BORN 1887

LATVIA

ED L.

He was in his fifties by that time, and he was starting to slow down. Though he would create a number of new pieces for his attraction and though he had yet to build the massive walls that would eventually surround his compound and the two-story tower he would live in, Ed considered himself finished with his "Rock Gate Park."

He was also finished with Agnes Scuffs.

The move may have played a part symbolically in Ed's decision to put the lost love of his life behind him at last.

"I left her down at Florida City and don't talk about her anymore," he told Orval Irwin, after Irwin had not heard Ed mention his 'Sweet Sixteen' for a while.[12] By this time in his life whatever hopes he had held for her return and his plans for a wife and family, probably had disappeared. Instead, they became part of the show for paying customers, a bit of romance he used to add luster to his giant megalith. Ed even "rearranged and renamed some new stone areas of the castle,"[13] further suggesting that, even though he continued to tell the story of his Sweet Sixteen to the tourists, he had moved on emotionally as well as physically.

At the new address, Ed applied himself first to building the eight-foot walls that surround the courtyard, giving his new home much more of a "castle-like" appearance than it had in Florida City. Given that the new place was in a much more heavily traveled area, building the high walls—which are three feet thick—made a lot of sense. The stone slabs he used in constructing the wall weighed as much as twenty-nine tons each. He filled the spaces between the stones with much smaller rocks "placed so perfectly that no light shows through."

The tops and sides of the walls are amazingly flat and even as well. Given the jagged and brittle nature of coral rock—and the primitive nature of Ed's tools—the precision of the walls is stunning. They stand tightly, side by side, their tops so even the casual viewer could be forgiven for assuming they'd been shaped by a machine.

Again, the question arises as to how Ed was able to move these giant stones and set them into place so precisely.

He added a number of new pieces to Rock Gate Park as well, including a barbeque area and well, his Polaris telescope and a sundial.

The new pieces are easy to distinguish from the older ones. The Homestead coral Ed was working with now was of a slightly different color and texture than what he'd quarried at Florida City—a slightly darker gray, more jagged and pitted, as opposed to the smooth, almost white stone he'd previously excavated.

Many of the Homestead pieces also are more sophisticated in design. Comparing the Floriday City obelisk, for example, to the new Polaris telescope, it is clear that Ed had honed his craft. The lines on the telescope are straight, narrowing a bit toward the top, while the obelisk has an oddly unbalanced shape. The placement of the new pieces was also very precise. The huge gates he constructed moved with an easy touch and were uncannily balanced, a clear step up from the rocking chairs he had fashioned in Florida City.

The two-story tower that became his living quarters was also a tremendous improvement on the pine shack he had lived in at Florida City. (He did, however, move the shack to the new property, locating it behind the castle, just outside the east wall. It is no longer there.)

He worked, too, on his presentation to the tourists.

In the wide stone doorway leading to his 'Rock Gate Park,' Ed rigged a bell with a rope. A sign next to it ordered the visitor to "Ring Twice" for a tour. If the visitor rang it only once, or more than twice, Ed would not answer. .

In *Korallu Pils*, author Andris Stavro speculated that Ed used the sign to be sure that his visitor could read English; if the visitor could not, he might be a Russian agent out to get Ed.

This theory seems doubtful.

More likely, ringing twice signaled to Ed that the person at the door wanted a tour—and had paid the admission fee, which meant Ed had good reason to stop whatever he was doing.

Two rings also implied that the visitor was willing and able to follow orders. Ed gave a tour very much on his own terms and at his own pace. By ringing twice, the visitor tacitly agreed that Ed was lord of this manor and would determine how things were done here. Questions were forbidden until the tour was completed.

Homestead resident Ruth Campbell, who took her first tour of the castle in the early forties, recalls that Ed gave the tour as he wanted to give it. "He was so proud, and he would take you around and tell you about each piece that he had," she says. "He wanted you to see everything, and he would tell you about each fantasy, every idea, all of his pieces, the bedroom, the barbeque pit, everything. He wanted to tell you in detail about every single thing he had there. And you didn't go ahead of him either. Or he would brush you off for sure."[14]

If Ed could be somewhat dictatorial while giving his tour, he

The bell and the sign at the front door to Rock Gate. Visitors who did not ring twice were not given a tour.

managed, at least, to be a benign dictator. To a person, locals recall his generosity and his personal attention.

"He was very nice to us," M.C. Bardsley says, recalling a tour she took with her Girl Scout troop in the late 1930s. "He would take all afternoon to talk to us. We were twelve or thirteen years old. He was shy, but he was comfortable with us, maybe because we were just kids."[15]

Signers of the 1955 affidavits recall not just Ed's personal manner, but his almost uncanny ability to recognize people who had been to

Children loved to visit Rock Gate, and the child-like Ed seemed to be more comfortable with them than with their parents.

the castle before—even when it had been a long time since the visit.

"Ed never forgot a face," wrote one woman. "Having been to his place once, and return with another group of friends, Ed would point to each one and say if you had been there before.... [He]was a clever little man." [16]

"Had a wonderful memory," declared Mrs. C.F. Waldron on her affidavit. "We visited his place in Fla. City & years afterwards visited the one on Highway 1 & he knew us. He never charged admission to those who had gone in once."[17]

When a tour began, Ed moved with great excitement from piece to piece, chattering away about how he created each one. "He had a very high-pitched voice, " Ruth Campbell recalled. "You had to sort of tune in to hear and understand everything he said."[18] One thing Campbell does not remember Ed having is a thick accent. He had a slight accent, which had been softened by having lived in America for so many years.

After the bombing of Pearl Harbor on December 7, 1941, America began mobilizing for war. Part of that effort involved creating Homestead Army Airfield, a military base that opened on September 16, 1942 (it is now called Homestead Joint Air Reserve Base). Initially used as a transport station for flights to the African theater of action, it quickly became one of the most important flight training facilities in the country. It also was used to house prisoners of war.[19]

The war seems to have served as an impetus for Ed—after thirty years of living in America—to apply for US citizenship. He may have feared that, as the citizen of a foreign country, he could be arrested, sent to an internment camp, or even deported. Those fears were not without reason. As the political pot boiled more and more fiercely in Europe and Asia in the late 1930s, the US government began putting under surveillance what were known as "potentially dangerous persons." Peopled with Japanese, Italian, and/or German backgrounds began to be viewed with suspicion; Russians, though technically our allies, were not to be trusted either. When war was declared, the FBI and INS agents began rounding up "enemy aliens" and deporting or interning them. One such camp was located in nearby Miami.[20]

Having witnessed the violence—sometimes random and unwarranted—during his years in Latvia, Ed was no doubt worried about his own status.

In fact, according to some stories that circulated at the time, the US government had already paid Ed a visit regarding his radio antennae—the strange strand of wire Ed had strung across the wall of the castle from the top of the crescent moon to the star on the obelisk. The radio was allegedly interfering with radio signals at the nearby Air Force base. Some say the callers were FBI agents. Others say the FBI sent for the sheriff, who knew Ed. Still others say the sheriff and agents went together.

In his book *Mr. Can't Is Dead*, Orval Irwin ascribes the visit to his father, a deputy sheriff. Irwin recounts the story of Ed showing his father how the wires were connected to his simple crystal radio set, which made it possible for him to listen to both music and news for free and that the copper wires were a simple, homemade radio antennae.

"My father chuckled as he told me about it," Irwin writes. "I think that it was one investigation that he and the agent thoroughly enjoyed."[21]

But other locals tell a different story. They say that Ed was warned about the agents and sheriff coming to investigate and was able to convince them that his apparatus was harmless.[22] Though Irwin claimed his father "chuckled" about the confrontation with the authorities, one has to wonder if the FBI agents laughed too, or if their suspicions were entirely allayed by Ed's claim that he was grabbing only the songs of the day out of the air.

Conspiracy theorists believe Ed was warned—and that, in fact, he was doing something more with that radio than simply listening to music and news. Some believe, in fact, that Ed was already the subject of government suspicion by the time war broke out. For reasons that had nothing to do with the castle he had built.

✦　✦　✦　✦　✦

During the war years, the governments of every country in the conflict were exploring possibilities of new and more devastating weapons, from the V-1 rocket to the atomic bomb to laser-beam death rays. Technology—and the scientists who were able to apply it to the construction of these destructive new devices—moved to the forefront of awareness among all civilized nations, and the intelligence agencies charged with the security of those countries.

There are those who believe that Ed was targeted for suspicion by the U.S. government because of a patent he had applied for in the 1930s. A patent for what he called a magnetic generator, which some people believe was, in fact, a perpetual-motion machine.

The US Patent Office has no record of applications dating back to that timeframe; the records for issued patents, which date back into the nineteenth century, list no one by the name of Edward Leedskalnin.

Did Ed ever apply for a patent? Was his idea rejected? Was it judged unworthy of a patent? There is no way to know for sure now. Conspiracy theorists believe that the perpetual-motion generator, which could supply the world with free energy, would have undermined the utility and oil companies and for that reason the patent was not granted. Others say the government took note of the idea and came to Homestead to try to take it from Ed.

The truth of those rumors aside, Ed certainly must have had an inkling—perhaps more than that—of how suspicious the facts about his life could appear to others. He spoke both German and Russian; he had never become a U.S. citizen; and within his living tower, he had constructed his very own, very powerful radio transmitter.

The decision to become a citizen, seen in that light, was a pragmatic one.

A gaunt-looking Ed stands next to the homemade winch he used to help move his giant stones.

On the form he spelled his name as we know it today. He described himself as having a fair complexion, blue eyes, and brown hair. His weight he declared as 120 pounds. He was now—according to the form at least—5'7" tall.

His naturalization papers were officially awarded on May 17, 1944; he carved the numbers from those papers on the doorway to his second-floor living area shortly after he received them. 7129 (the petition number on the certificate of naturalization), and 6105195 (the certificate number itself). Visitors to the castle can still see these numbers—very small and now faint—cut into the rock doorway.

His reasons for carving them, as always, are a subject of debate.

The simplest answer appeals to some: Ed etched the numbers associated with his new citizenship in his home as an act of patriotism, an act of pride and faith in his new country.

Others feel he feared further questioning by the government or perhaps arrest, even deportment. Ed wanted the number close at hand and in full view in case he—or those sent to apprehend him—had need of them.

Other explanations are more exotic.

A rumor circulated that the numbers appeared as part of a message left by Ed announcing "The Secret to the Universe is 71296105105" (even though the first part of that message—"The Secret to the Universe is"—does not appear anywhere in Ed's living quarters). Another rumor then made the rounds stating that Ed told someone on his deathbed that the numbers revealed the secret to the universe. This version, too, has no evidence to support it (there is no record of anyone visiting Ed in the weeks before his death).

A Web site called Code144.com attracted attention in the paranormal community when it posted a mathematically complex formula using those numbers, alleging they contained "the Secret to the Universe." The site's director was not dissuaded from believing the formula significant even after he learned that the number was taken from Ed's naturalization certificate. On the site he stated:

"It appears as though Edward Leedskalnin was able to have some influence over the numbers he was issued, allowing him to integrate the numbers as another multifaceted clue at Coral Castle. Many people will prefer at this point to believe that there is no other meaning to these numbers and that is understandable, though I would strongly encourage readers not to underestimate the greatness of the forces at work.[23]"

Given the passion and, in some cases, the erudition with which the proponents of what is called "ultrascience" state their beliefs, our goal is not to undermine or ridicule, but in this case, the ultrascientists clearly seem to be off base.

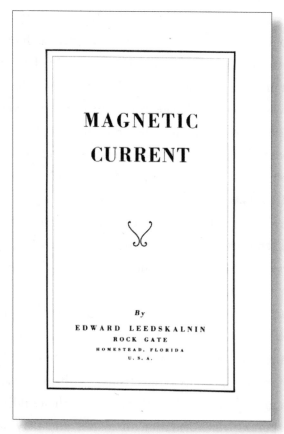

MAGNETIC

CURRENT

By

EDWARD   LEEDSKALNIN
ROCK   GATE
HOMESTEAD, FLORIDA
U. S. A.

The cover of *Magnetic Current,* the booklet Ed published himself that contains his mystifying theories on electromagnetism.

In the years after the war, Ed added no new pieces to the castle. Instead, he focused on his experiments with electricity, which he discussed in detail in a booklet titled *Magnetic Current.*

We don't know where Ed learned about the subject, though the 1955 affidavits offer a clue. Shopkeeper Howard B. Johnson declared, "I have sold Ed at various times scientific magazines and on numerous occasions talked with him about his work. He invariably would ride his bicycle into Homestead each after afternoon...."[24]

Others stated that when they visited Rock Gate Park during this time, Ed would talk to them about his experiments with radio and electricity. He may even have begun including discussion of magnetic current at this point in his tour. In an affidavit, Herman J. McConnell writes, "I first met Edward Leedskalnin late in 1943 when he showed me the Rock Gate...and on one occasion in 1946 while there he showed us some of his experiments that resulted in his writing...*Magnetic Current*."[25]

He published the booklet himself in August of 1945 and sold copies at Rock Gate Park. In October of that year he published a long "advertisement" for the booklet in the *Miami Daily News*, a densely written essay more than a thousand words long in which he explained his theories about magnetic current, redefining the nature of the atom and of matter itself.

In the booklet, Ed blasts scholars and scientists, calling them "the men with the long hair." He dismisses prevailing theories of physics and most other natural sciences, from botany to biology. His theories replace the atom—specifically electrons—with magnets. He writes that the magnetic north and south poles "are the building blocks of nature's perpetual transformation of matter and they are so small they can pass through everything." This allowed him to redefine both the law of gravity and the nature of electricity. He saw the former as a force created by magnetic energy concentrated at the earth's core. The pull of that magnetic force on the magnets that fill everything accounts for what we know as gravity.

In the ad he also referred to "the perpetual motion holder which I made," the device mentioned earlier as a potential reason for the government targeting Ed, and his work.

One would think such a claim would send scientists from throughout the world scurrying to Ed's door, but he seems to have been mostly ignored.

Mainstream scientists scoff at Ed's work, which has never been accepted as legitimate. Some see this as at least partially due to his inability to articulate his thoughts; lacking a background in physics and mathematics, he was unable to express in a meaningful way the discoveries he made in his experiments.

It is also possibile that in publishing the booklet Ed was trying once more to affirm his own genius. People who visited the castle always mentioned the pride he took in his work. Having finished that work, he sought a new way of awing his neighbors, the tourists, the world. He would be the next Einstein, the next Tesla—a world-famous scientist, the person who discovered the nature of all things. His rejection of nearly every accepted tenet within the discipline suggests that he was looking for ways to prove everyone wrong, to make a breakthrough like Einstein's theory of relativity, to show that he was smarter than the rest of the world.

How many copies of the booklet he sold—at one dollar each—is not recorded.

✦　✦　✦　✦　✦

By the late 1940s, Ed was in his sixties and not looking well. Photos from the period show he had lost weight, becoming very thin. Though his face remains firm and stoic, his cheekbones protrude, and his body looks emaciated.

His diet consisted mostly of the vegetables he grew on his property, along with rabbits he would trap. Locals recall him buying crackers and sardines. Museum guide John Landgrave says that Ed grew more than he could eat and bartered his abundance for the foods he wanted.[26]

It was a rare event for Ed to accept a dinner invitation. In a number of the affidavits, people remark that Ed would not take help or a favor or a meal or even a car ride from anyone. Annie Biggers Couch writes, "I have known Ed since 1938 personally, but he would never

A rare candid shot of Ed during his final years.

accept invitations for dinners as he preferred his own simple diet."[27]

In his final years, Ed's refusals began to soften. Long-time Homestead resident Frances Boysen recalls eating Thanksgiving dinner with Ed in 1949 and 1950 at the home of Casper Williams, the grandfather of both her daughters-in-law. She doesn't recall much about Ed, saying that he seemed "very ordinary" and also very shy.

"The family would talk but he didn't talk," she says. "He would sit there and eat. If you asked him a question he would answer but otherwise, he was quiet."[28] Boysen had moved with her family to the area in 1948, when she was twenty-three years old. She did not visit the castle and had no interest in it at the time, focusing instead on socializing with people her own age. She does not know if Ed had been to Casper's house before that first Thanksgiving.

"For some reason I assumed that he had eaten there before," she says. "Because they lived right on old Dixie Highway not too far from where he moved his things. I think they knew him more from just being around."

She says that the Williams family was friendly to everyone and very sociable. None of them were particularly close to Ed.

"I don't think Ed had any real close friends," she says. "Nobody knew him that well, but everybody knew him."

It's possible that Ed began accepting invitations like the Williams in his final years not because he was growing less self-sufficient, but because he was getting lonely.

Support for this theory comes from *Korallu Pils*. In the book, Andris Stavro presents a letter that Ed wrote to his brother Otto on October 9, 1950. The letter arrived in Latvia in November. Ed wrote (in Latvian):

> I am your brother Edward. I am sending you two pictures of my house which I have made. I have forgotten how to write in Latvian. It has been 35 years since I have gotten a letter from Latvia. Send me a letter and let me know how you are.[29]

Ed may have begun to sense his failing health. He wanted to connect with his family, to tell them what he had done.

Otto's son Evald took the letter to the local leaders of the Communist party: he feared that receiving a letter from America would bring his family under suspicion. Evald was an active member of the party and also feared he would be kicked out as a result of the letter.[30]

If Otto replied to his brother, no record exists. If he did respond, it's likely that Evald did not send the letter, perhaps even destroyed it. He didn't want an ongoing correspondence between his father and someone in the United States, no matter how harmless.

The failure to make a connection with his brother—to rekindle a

Ed's bedroom, showing the magazines he read about science and electricity.

relationship with family, and home—would only have increased Ed's feelings of loneliness and isolation. Those feelings are touchingly illustrated by a description from a local man named Samuel L. Herndon, who writes: "He made a rather curious picture peering over the wall watching traffic on the highway with only sun helmet and eyes showing."[31]

Quite an image: Ed peering over the top of his walls, which he had built to protect himself and insure his privacy but also a physical manifestation of the walls he erected around himself out of fear or paranoia or timidity. In the end, he finds himself looking out, perhaps wondering if anyone is looking back.

In his affidavit, Herndon also says that at their last meeting, Ed said he was planning to rewrite the textbooks on electrical theory. But Ed ran out of time for that ambitious project. His health, never good, grew worse. He continued to lose weight. Some say he was suffering from stomach cancer. Others believe that he had simply stopped eating and was dying of malnutrition.

In the Leedskalnin legend, the tale of his death is always the same: Ed put a sign on the door of Rock Gate announcing that he was "going to the hospital." Three days later he was dead. Like much of the "facts" in the Leedskalnin legend, however, this story isn't true.

His death certificate reveals the real facts.

Ed spent twenty-eight days dying at Jackson Hospital in Miami, checking himself in on November 9, 1951. Given what many people have said in interviews and on the 1955 affidavits about Ed not accepting rides from his neighbors, he probably took a bus to the hospital.

Despite reports that he had stomach cancer, the truth is that Ed was suffering from pyelonephritis, a kidney infection, which, if untreated, can spread to the bloodstream and infect the entire body.[32] The death certificate notes that the condition existed with an "absess," meaning that Ed probably arrived at the hospital too late to survive the illness.

The certificate also notes that the condition was complicated by a "cerebral hemorrhage." Ed had suffered a stroke—perhaps before he left the castle, perhaps at the hospital. The final cause of death is noted as "uremia;" failure of the kidneys, as a result of the infection and abscess.

On Friday December 7, 1951, at 2:50 in the morning, Ed Leedskalnin died at the age of sixty-four. He had been gone long enough that surely people in Homestead must have noticed his absence, though he spent so much time alone perhaps they didn't pay much attention. Ironically, a small piece about him appeared in the *Homestead Leader-Enterprise* on the day he died. On page five (of an eight-page issue) of the weekly newspaper, in a round-up section called "In and Around Homestead," locals found the following squib: "Edward Leedskalnin of Rock Gate on U.S. 1 has been in Jackson Memorial Hospital for the past week in a very serious condition."

If anyone read the notice and thought about taking a trip to Miami to visit him, they were, of course, already too late.

No one, in any case, came to identify the body.

Ed was buried the following Wednesday at Miami Memorial Park. There is no record of who—if anyone—attended the burial.

A short obituary appeared in the *Miami News*, where Ed had published both his long advertisements for Rock Gate and for *Magnetic Current*. It read:

"Edward Leedskalnin died yesterday in a Miami hospital. He leaves no survivors. Philbrick's Miami funeral home will announce funeral arrangements."

The generic nature of the obituary makes clear that no one at the newspaper recognized the name or its association with Rock Gate.

Ed was treated more kindly by the local press. The front page of the December 14, 1951, edition of the *Redland District News* included a short article titled "Death Takes Creator of 'Rock Gate.'" It was not

In this abode the experiments with magnets were made and the results recorded by Ed. L. in 1945.

ROCK GATE • Homestead, Florida, U. S. A.

EDWARD LEEDSKALNIN

The Man Above—He Is the One Who Made the Place

PRINTED BY THE FRANKLIN PRESS, INC.——SEPTEMBER, 1950

A postcard from Rock Gate, one of Ed's final marketing efforts.

treated as headline news. In fact, it ran under an article announcing a holiday concert performed by the high school band.

The article read, in part:

"A native of Lithuania, Leedskalnin came to South Dade 30 years ago from the State of Washington. He leaves no known survivors." The piece went on to describe Rock Gate and note that "Ed's Place" originally was located in Florida City.

The *Leader-Enterprise* offered a bit more coverage the same day, in an article that appeared at the bottom of page one under the title "Death Takes Leedskalnin, Carver of Monolithic Wonders at Ed's Place." After announcing Ed's death, the article states, "Although he had been a patient at the hospital since Nov. 9, few of his friends and neighbors here knew of his illness." Following a series of paragraphs describing Rock Gate, the article closed by stating that "officers of First National Bank of Miami, named executors of the estate, took charge of funeral arrangement, and were this week trying to track down nieces and nephews who will inherit his property."

The mysterious Edward Leedskalnin was dead.

But his story—and that of the fantastic monument he'd built—was far from over.

Ed's death certificate.

A bathing beauty reclines in the Crescent of the East
at Coral Castle in the 1950s.

6

A NEW LIFE FOR
THE CORAL CASTLE

With Ed's death, the castle's future was left in doubt. For his friends and neighbors, for the tourists and visitors, hearing about the amazing stone sculptures from the odd little man who built them was part of the charm of the place. Would Rock Gate remain an attraction, or would Ed's many years of labor be consigned to the bulldozers? No one was sure. His death had been sudden and unexpected. The Homestead folks weren't sure what to do. Some hoped that the state would take on the property and keep it open as an historic landmark.[1]

The First National Bank of Miami was named the executor of the will. Ed owned little other than the castle and the surrounding property, which he had bequeathed to his nephew, Harry Leedskalnin, who was living at the time in Detroit. Little is known about Harry, allegedly the grandson of Ed's brother Otto. The younger Leedskalnin had written to Ed in the fall of 1950 from Grand Rapids—a letter which may in turn have sparked Ed's own decision to write to Otto. Harry had come to the US after World War II, in which he had fought in the German army, having been pressed into service, as were a number of Latvian men, to bolster the failing German war effort. By the time the war ended, Harry was in a prisoner-of-war camp. He came to the US in 1948 as part of the Displaced Persons Act, which allowed admission of war refugees, overriding government quotas.[2] After coming to the US as a displaced person, he read about Ed and the Coral Castle in a newspaper; according to some, in fact, he even visited Ed in Homestead in early 1951.[3]

Harry, however, was unable to take possession of Rock Gate.

He had no money to run it—or to pay the overdue property taxes due to the state. He was forced to surrender Rock Gate Park to the State of Florida for sale to someone else.

That someone else turned out to be Julius Levin, a wealthy, thirty-nine-year-old Chicago jeweler who had retired to Miami in 1952. Harry and his wife, Mary, signed over the property to Levin on April 7, 1953. (Harry would die later that year, perhaps from health issues related to his war experience.) The deal was finalized on May 1, nearly a year and a half after Ed left to go to the hospital.[4] According to his obituary in the *Chicago Sun-Times* in 1990, Levin bought the property without knowledge that "a neglected castle" stood on it.[5]

In the interim, Rock Gate Park had languished. It had not been open for business or cared for since October of 1951, and we have no record of how long Ed struggled with illness before boarding the bus for the hospital. By the time the Levins arrived, weeds had grown up around the stones. Wild vines spread like exotic spider webs over the walls, the chairs, the planets, and Ed's tower. The tropical plants, flowers, and trees inside and around the castle had flourished uncontrolled.

Fortunately, the new owner fell in love with the place. Though he bought the property unaware of the incredible monument that occupied a corner of it, Julius Levin set out to revive and reopen Rock Gate. He cleared the wild growth and landscaped the entire area. He planted bougainvillea and other tropical plants, giving the castle a natural splendor it had never had before. He hired a neighbor, Francis

New owner Julius Levin loved Coral Castle and made
many improvements to the grounds.

Wilson, to run the place, and employed her husband, Marion, to build
a gift shop and entry area. It was Levin who hired Bodil Lowe to gen-
erate publicity for the castle, in the course of which she gathered the
many affidavits from people in Homestead and Florida City who were
familiar with both Ed and the castle's history. Levin himself also interviewed many of the locals, collecting their stories and recollections
about his new attraction.

Within the year, Rock Gate Park was open for business again.[6]

(Left to right): Francis Wilson, Julius Levin, and Bodil Lowe, who collectively operated Coral Castle from the early 1950s through the 1970s.

The 1950s were a good time to be in the tourist industry—particularly the Florida tourist industry. Gas was cheap, the economy was strong, and the average middle-class family could afford to drive to the Sunshine State from anywhere in the East, Southeast, and Midwest. By the late 1950s, the new interstate highway system made that drive easier than ever. A "Florida vacation" became a familiar symbol for the country's new prosperity.

New attractions sprang up to entice the throng of travelers. From Caribbean Gardens to Busch Gardens to Cape Coral Gardens to Tiki Gardens, from Storyland to Floridaland to Treasureland, from Silver Springs to Sunshine Springs to Weeki Wachee Spring, from Pirates

World to Pioneer City, from the Miami Seaquarium to the Aquatarium, from Gatorama to the Florida Citrus Tower, the state brimmed with new entertainment centers that, even if they were offering similar bits of kitschy Americana, were much more elaborate than their roadside predecessors had been.[7]

Competition for the tourist dollar was fierce. Julius Levin needed to ratchet up the marketing of the castle to a much higher level. And he did. He replaced Ed's dowdy, broken-English advertisements for "unusual accomplishment" with a good bit more pizzazz. Some locals may have complained about the commercialization of Ed's Place, but others saw the need to add some oomph to entice tourists and keep the castle a going concern.

A brochure from the early '50s beckons in bold, capital letters, "VISIT THE CORAL CASTLE OF FLORIDA AT ROCK GATE PARK" above a photo of a young woman in a one-piece bathing suit standing on Ed's crescent moon, her hands raised ecstatically above her head. Below the image, the reader is warned that "Your Vacation Won't Be Complete" unless it includes a visit to the castle. On the back of the brochure, which includes a map to what is still called "Rock Gate Park," the reader learns that "The Coral Castle of Florida" was "Created for the Love of a Woman." The word "Romantic" appears in a seductive cursive font at the bottom.

The copy inside the brochure—which wraps around more photos of bathing-suited beauties—is similarly florid, trumpeting claims like, "...it can be compared ONLY to such wonders of the world as the Pyramids of Cheops at Giza, the Stonehenge in England, and the Colosseum of Rome."[8]

This brochure is quite possibly the first published mention of the name "Coral Castle," though at this point, it's merely a descriptor for Rock Gate Park. Soon after, however, the latter name was dropped, and Levin officially christened the attraction Coral Castle—a memo-

A photo shoot at Coral Castle in the late 1950s.

A model stands on the Florida table during a photo shoot in the late 1950s.

rable, alliterative moniker that conjured images of tropical splendor.

In ads from the mid '50s, Levin molded a new marketing campaign around the catchphrase "Love Turned to Stone." One ad features the face of a winsome young girl framed in a locket next to a drawing of the castle tower and the Polaris telescope. It captured both the romance of lost love and the power of the structure itself. Ed's lost-long Sweet Sixteen lived on.[9]

This campaign soon gave way to full-color advertisements and postcards in which even the stones were colorized to look pink, purple, and red. Tourists drawn by these photos were perhaps a bit disappointed to pull up to the castle and find only gray stone. And though it's unlikely that Coral Castle thrilled kids hoping to see alligators, parrots, monkeys, roller coasters, water-ski stunts and glass-bottom boats, Ed's huge rocks, and the amazing story behind them, brought in enough customers to keep the place going.

The *Miami Herald* published several articles about Coral Castle in the late 1950s, including a striking black-and-white photo feature that included beautiful models perched on Ed's sculptures. The photo layouts make vivid the castle's charm and power in a brilliant light that Ed never quite captured with his Brownie box camera. And the tone of these photos is much more inviting, frankly, without Ed looking stiff and dour in his black suit. The castle seems to be a lush, ancient temple of love—a place any traveler would want to visit.

Levin soon developed a new business, which he called the Tropical Florida Vacation Plan. Based in Miami, where the Levins lived, the Tropical Florida Vacation Plan offered tourists a structured day trip to a number of attractions. They boarded a bus and visited Monkey Jungle, Parrot Jungle, and a few other attractions, including Coral Castle.[10]

"He said people were more enthralled by Coral Castle than any of the other places," recalls Levin's daughter, Linda Leibsker. She also recalls that her father loved the castle and spent nearly every day there. The rest of the family often joined him on weekends. Liebsker remembers climbing on the stones as a child in the 1950s, and watching tourists work their way through the tours. Her favorite place to play was the wooden shack behind the castle—Ed's living quarters from his Florida City days.

Throughout the decade, and on into the 1960s, Julius Levin continued to work on the landscaping and horticultural aspects of the castle. He devoted his best efforts to making Coral Castle more beautiful than it had ever been. He saw "Ed's place" as a unique piece of folk art and did his best to ensure it would be preserved.

Unfortunately, he couldn't find a way to make the castle profitable.

Family members, says his daughter, thought his obsession bordered on folly.

"We thought it was crazy," she says. "It never made any money. If someone couldn't afford the admission he'd let them in for free. The family kind of encouraged him to sell it."[11]

The unearthly charm of the castle captivated others as well—mythmakers in their own right, who by the end of the decade had put Ed's place to uses the little man could never in his wildest dreams have imagined.

Kitschy America, by the 1950s, was not only on display from the Florida roadside. The 1950s, in addition to the tourist boom, also saw an explosion from the movie screen—B-movies, which included fantasy and science fiction films that were often little more than excuses to show leggy starlets in skimpy bathing suits or skimpy futuristic costumes.

One of those films was 1958's *Wild Women of Wongo*, directed by James L. Wolcott, which features leggy starlets running around in skimpy, primitive costumes. The film is also notable for its music soundtrack—the same soundtrack that would later be used in 1959's *Plan 9 from Outer Space*, often picked as the worst B-movie ever made—and for the fact that it used Coral Castle as the setting for some of its scenes. Filmfanatic.org declared the title the best part of the movie. "The script and dialogue are inane…and there are countless laughably incompetent moments."

In 1961, filmmakers visited Coral Castle again, this time to film *Nude on the Moon*, directed by long-time sexploitation auteur Doris Wishman. The movie tells the story of two American scientists who funded their own trip to the moon, where they find a tropical paradise inhabited by topless women. The erstwhile space explorers watch the 'Moon Goddess' bathe in Ed's tub and sit on Ed's throne chair. Other parts of the castle function at various times as perches for the moon's half-naked female inhabitants.

Glenn Erickson at dvdtalk.com warned people not to "...confuse it with a movie."

Dvdverdict.com, on the other hand, pronounced *Nude on the Moon* "one of the best of the Doris Wishman nudist camp classics," citing "the indubitably bizarre surroundings...[which] look like a combination Mayan spa and Morlock granary."

In 1966, director Herschell Gordon Lewis used Coral Castle as the setting for the children's film *Jimmy the Boy Wonder*; kiddiematinee. com called the film "some sort of evil LSD home movie for kids."

In 1982 two low-budget Mexican films starring a then-famous masked wrestler named El Santo (Rodolfo Guzmán Huerta), who was sixty-four years old at the time, were shot simultaneously using a number of South Florida locations, including Coral Castle. *La furia de los Karatecas* (Fury of the Karate Killers) and *El Puno de la Muerte* (Fist of Death), though not as cringe-worthy as the movies that preceded them, did not exactly earn the type of respect Ed would have wanted for his life's work.[12]

Coral Castle fared much better on the small screen, where it was presented seriously as a mysterious place worthy of the public's attention. It first appeared on television in the summer of 1957 on a popular show called *You Asked for It,* in which viewers sent in requests to see unusual and even bizarre people, places, and situations. (The requests to put Coral Castle on the show had come from Julius Levin himself, who hoped that national exposure would spark interest in his attraction.)[13]

The castle next appeared, and most famously, on January 24, 1981, when it was featured on an episode of *In Search Of,* a show hosted by Leonard Nimoy, best known as *Star Trek*'s Mr. Spock.[14] The half-

Publicity posters for two of the low-budget films made at Coral Castle.

hour, documentary-style program ran from 1976 through 1982, each episode exploring a mysterious or paranormal subject. The episode on Coral Castle was titled "The Castle of Secrets." As of this writing, it can be found in its entirety on YouTube. With its eerie soundtrack and Nimoy's stentorian voice, the show offers a number of captivating moments, even for viewers already familiar with the castle and its creator. Several locals from Homestead are interviewed, among them Francis Wilson, who Julius Levin had hired to run the castle, and Bodil Lowe, who had gathered all those affidavits for Levin back in the 1950s. Both agreed that Ed was a sweet, if mysterious, guy.

The show's producer neglects to mention that each was employed by the castle—but from the vantage point of thirty years later, it's fascinating to put faces to the names of those associated with the castle's history.

The show offers its share of faulty information, as well as a few dramatic reenactments that have little connection to the truth. In a scene recreating Ed's move from Florida City to Homestead, Bob Biggers leaves his truck and walks around a corner—only to turn back and see that Ed, in a matter of seconds, has already loaded his giant stones onto the truck.

No one claims that Ed was able to move the rocks quite that fast!

Much more powerful—and believable—are the show's attempt to demonstrate the enormity of Ed's accomplishment. A construction crew sweats and strains to cut a slab of coral rock while using a diamond-tipped power saw, a far more powerful piece of equipment than any Ed ever possessed. Using a six-hundred-horsepower crane, the crew attempts to lift the freshly cut stone slab, which sags and sways in the air while nearly toppling the crane. Of course, with a single chain wrapped around the middle of the stone, the crew makes no attempt to use balance or leverage, but the demonstration does capture the difficulty—and enormity—of the challenge Ed faced in maneuvering such gigantic pieces.

The most fascinating moment of the show, however, comes from watching footage of Ed himself. Taken from a home movie found in the closet of a local person, the footage, which is grainy and lasts only about ten seconds, shows a picnic at what appears to be Ed's Place in Florida City, in the late 1920s or early 1930s. Ed and his neighbors rock in the stone chairs; he points up at the obelisk, and then, for a brief moment, the camera focuses closely on Ed. We see a boyish, embarrassed smile, as his hand brushes his hair away from his forehead This fleeting image shows us, for the first time, the real Edward Leedskalnin—not the formal, rigid, unsmiling man he posed as in the pictures he took himself, but the one who his neighbors always described as gracious and genial.

Joe Bullard, author of *Waiting for Agnes*, a fictionalized retelling of Ed's story and considered one of the cornerstone books on the subject,[15] cites the *In Search Of* episode as his introduction to Coral Castle. A native of Florida, Bullard was surprised to learn that such a mysterious place existed in his home state.

"After seeing it on TV, I was fascinated by the place," Bullard says. "I had to go down there and see it for myself."

The trip he took from his home in northern Florida to Homestead changed Bullard's life. In Homestead, he met an elderly local man named J.T. Bullard (no relation) who told him many stories about Ed and the castle (some of which have been already mentioned here), sparking the research he then spent years of his life doing before writing his novel.

Other shows with formats similar to *In Search Of* followed suit. Coral Castle was soon featured on *That's Incredible* and *Unsolved Mysteries*, along with several local programs in South Florida. Tour guides say that many of the castle's visitors, having learned of the place on television, decide to come and see it for themselves.

The renewed attention gave the castle a new credibility, even among those who reject views ascribing supernatural origins and symbolism to the structure. Compared to Florida's Disney World, Universal Studios, and other mega-attractions, Coral Castle may seem small and antiquated, but it also seems authentic—a startling and mysterious achievement created by one man through hard work over the course of many years, a truly "unusual accomplishment."

In a clear case of poor timing, Julius Levin sold Coral Castle just ten days before the episode of *In Search Of* introduced the entire country to this amazing place, transferring the deed to Coral Castle, Inc. on January 14, 1981. In her father's *Sun-Times* obituary, Linda Leibsker suggests that her father had no regrets.

"He didn't run it to make a lot of money," she says. "He saw the artistic side of the place." The family had been telling him to sell it for years, and financial concerns were raised in the press as early as 1966.[16] Every attraction located south of Orlando had suffered after Walt Disney World opened in October 1971. As one frustrated motel owner complained, "It was as if someone had built a wall across the middle of the state."[17] When Levin's health began to fail in the 1970s, he decided, at last, that his family was right.

Coral Castle, Inc. maintains ownership today.

In 1986, the story behind the castle received national attention from an unlikely source: pop singer Billy Idol, who, having heard about Ed and his "lost love," wrote and recorded a song called "Sweet Sixteen." Idol then filmed a video for the song at Coral Castle.

It's difficult to imagine how Ed would have reacted to seeing a shirtless pop singer with dyed-white hair seated in his throne chair. Perhaps he would have been delighted by the attention. Or, he might have fretted nervously about the castle courtyard, feeling that his property had been invaded by people who didn't really understand him. Or, less likely, he might have realized that he could have written a simple song to his Sweet Sixteen rather than devote thirty years of back-breaking labor to building an 1,100-ton monument for her. We'll never know for certain.

Coral Castle is today on the National Registry of Historic Places, insuring that it will be preserved despite continued commercial and residential growth in the area. Ed's masterpiece is safe from the bulldozers, which, through the years, have dismantled many of the once-popular roadside attractions in Florida that competed with Coral Castle for the attention, and dollars, of tourists.

Not even Mother Nature has been able to harm the place. On August 24, 1992, Hurricane Andrew, a Category 5, hit the Florida coast and demolished most of Homestead. It was one of the strongest hurricanes in American history and absolutely devastated the area except for Coral Castle, which did not budge an inch. The gift shop/admission area was wiped out, as were most of the buildings in Homestead, but the castle itself remained, for the most part, unperturbed. A tall palm tree collapsed onto one of the outer walls, cutting a six-inch scratch on the coral, but no other damage was found. In fact, the castle became a support station, of sorts, for the clean-up operation led by Bravo Company of the 307th Engineers Batallion, 82nd Airborne Division. The engineers even camped on the castle property.[18]

The only real damage was done by someone in the days after the hurricane before the Army arrived. A looter—or curious scientist—used a chisel to cut through the rock to break open a latch on

Hurricane Andrew devastated much of Dade County in 1992,
but Ed's castle remained unharmed.

the second floor of the tower, in Ed's living quarters. The *New York Times* quoted caretaker Thomas Lowe, who said, "With all the force and everything of a hurricane, it took human beings to do this. That makes me mad."[19]

The sheer thickness and weight of the walls were more than a match for Hurricane Andrew. The porous texture of oolite probably helped too, allowing some of the wind's force to blow through. As Homesteaders surveyed the devastation of their property, they must have looked in envy at Ed Leedskalnin's house, which stood proud and tall, unchanged, unharmed.

It still stands now.

It will, in all likelihood, stand forever.

The mysterious Edward Leedskalnin

7

MYSTERIES AND
SECRETS

The Internet today hums with talk of Coral Castle and Ed Leedskalnin, most of it centered on the methods Ed used to construct
his masterpiece. Many conjectures exist, and their proponents are
zealous in their beliefs. Following is a roundup of the most popular
hypotheses. There are overlapping aspects to some of the arguments;
they're not mutually exclusive. Ed's ability to defy the laws of gravity,
for example, appears in a number of them. The energy grid theory,
meanwhile, is sometimes associated with UFOs and with magnetic current. Keeping them all clear isn't easy. At the same time it *is*
easy to be swayed when reading each one, because when nothing is
known, everything is possible.

Some ideas, however, do seem less likely than others.

The theory that states that Ed's grandfather (or uncle) met an old
wizard in Latvia, for example. According to this argument, the wizard knew the long-lost secrets of megalithic construction, secrets perhaps passed down from the Druids of Stonehenge or the Egyptians
of Giza. He gave this knowledge to the Leedskalnins. This theory,

however, does not consider why only Ed, of all the Leedskalnins, acted on the wizard's teachings—and then only after ten years of hard labor in America. Though it's difficult to put much credence in this idea, there are others worth considering more seriously.

The first of those is known as harmonic levitation.

In 2007, the *London Telegraph* published an article about research then happening at the University of St. Andrews in Scotland. Scientists there were briefly able to reverse the Casimir force, a theory in quantum physics that explains why atomic particles stick together. In the article, science editor Roger Highfield explains, "The force is due to neither electrical charge or gravity…but the fluctuations in all-pervasive energy fields in the intervening empty space between the objects." Two researchers—Ulf Leonhardt and Dr. Thomas Philbin—have used a "special lens" to cause the Casimir force "to repel rather than attract."

Researchers at Harvard University and the National Institute of Health reported a breakthrough in somewhat similar experiments in the January 2009 edition of *Nature: International Weekly Journal of Science*. In this study, the scientists were able to switch the Casimir force from attraction to repulsion through the use of fluids.

In his article "Scientists Use Quantum Mechanics to Levitate Microscopic Objects" in the January 8, 2009, edition of the *Tech Herald*, science writer Rich Bowden reported:

"The team, led by Federico Capasso, the Robert L. Wallace Professor of Applied Physics at Harvard's School of Engineering and Applied Science (SEAS), has yet to demonstrate the levitation but is confident the discovery will lead to the phenomenon.

"When two surfaces of the same material, such as gold, are separated by vacuum, air, or a fluid, the resulting force is always attractive,"

Levitation has always been the stuff of magic shows and fantasy, but did Ed Leedskalnin master the art in real life?

explained Capasso. However, when one of the two surfaces immersed in a fluid was replaced by one made of silica, the force immediately became repulsive."

These breakthroughs suggest that levitation—a levitation that does not break the existing laws of physics—is indeed possible, albeit levitation on the quantum level.

There are those who believe that levitation is the method by which Edward Leedskalnin was able to raise and precisely maneuver the massive coral rocks with which he built his castle.

They draw this inference from a story that began circulating at some point during Ed's years in Florida, one that was eventually quoted by author Frank Joseph in an article he wrote for *Fate* magazine. The story, as retold in *Fate*, declares that one night, some local teens snuck up on Ed and were able to actually witness him working on his castle.

They saw him levitating the huge rocks simply by singing to them.[1] A man named Fred Bullard (no relation to Joe, mentioned previously) was one of those kids. He told his daughter, Sharon, about the experience years later.[2]

According to some, the phenomenon those Florida teens witnessed is known as harmonic levitation, a process in which a certain sound pitch allegedly nullifies the gravitational pull on an object, allowing it to float in the air. The process sometimes is attributed to Tibetan monks, who are said to have mastered the art, and allegedly used it to float large rocks in the air and then move them to higher places. One of the better-known case studies is reported by Swedish writer Henry Kjelson in his essay "The Lost Techniques."[3] Kjelson writes about the experience of his friend, identified as "Dr. Jarl," who lived for a short time more with a group of Tibetan priests. Jarl testified that he witnessed chanting while beating on drums tuned to various pitches. After several minutes, the sounds caused rocks to lift into the air.

The para-scientific explanation of harmonic levitation is pretty simple: the condensed vibrations within a sound that achieves a certain pitch nullify the gravitational pull on an object, allowing it to break free and rise into the air above the surface on which it had rested. To achieve the levitation, the sound must achieve a certain frequency within a specific distance from the object.

In a documentary posted on YouTube, long-time Coral Castle guide Ray Ramirez speculates that the partially enclosed "redemption corner" at the castle may have been where Ed stood to hear and judge the frequencies he generated to cause the huge stones to lift into the air.

Others have theorized that the black box located at the top of the tall tripod from which Ed rigged the block and tackle used in constructing the castle may have contained frequency tuners that produced the tonal pitch necessary to reduce or eliminate gravitational pull, thus allowing Ed to lift the rocks and move them with equipment that otherwise would not be capable of the task.

If the story of the Homestead teens is true, perhaps what they assumed to be Ed singing to the rocks was actually the sound of the tuners, creating the frequency that would cause the rocks to float into position.

No evidence exists to confirm this theory—either about the box atop the tripod or about the validity of harmonic levitation. But the recent discoveries referred to above—discoveries made by mainstream scientists—suggest that levitation is no longer merely the stuff of science-fiction stories. Ed might have been far ahead of his time—and of ours as well.

✦ ✦ ✦ ✦ ✦

Ed works the chain on his tripod. Note the mysterious black box at the top, which some theorists believe holds the key to Ed's true methods of moving the stones.

Another possibility is that Ed, in building Coral Castle, had access to techniques created by ancient societies that, through time and conquest, have since been lost.

One intriguing theory is raised by a writer/researcher named Jim Solley in an essay titled "On Proving Ancient Megalith Construction."[4] Solly proposes that the pyramids and Coral Castle were built through the use of what he terms "ancient cement." He posits that by focusing on the difficulty in moving huge monoithic stones, theorists cannot solve the mystery. Instead, he says, they should question whether or not the stones truly are monoliths, meaning a single piece of stone. Solly believes that the Egyptians, and Ed, created the multi-ton stones from smaller, more manageable stones. By using cement, they could build the stones after they had placed them in position. He writes:

"Coral stone is one of Ed's many deceptions. It seems only to be an innocently convenient building material indigenous to the area, but it's not. It is rich in calcium carbonate, the primary chemical compound used to manufacture modern cement.[5]

Solly goes on to say that Ed's experience as a stonemason and also in the lumber industry would have taught him how to make wooden molds, into which he could first pour his cement, and then shape his stones. Much is made of the fact that no tool marks appear on Ed's sculptures and walls. Solly believes that any carved stone would exhibit some marks, but that if, instead, Ed used molds and cement, then no tool marks would be seen. He declares:

"As virtually no one [who visited the castle] would be impressed by missing tool marks, it is far more probable that missing tool marks is a byproduct of his technology than that he deliberately spent time ensuring that he left no tool marks.[6]

Solly's theory certainly explains one of the greatest mystery of the castle—the nine-ton rock gate that turns with the touch of a finger.

Recall that to create this piece, in the estimation of modern engineers, Ed had to not only find the perfect center of balance but then—with the primitive tools available to him—drill a perfect hole through the eight-foot-high stone, as he fed a metal shaft through it, balancing that shaft on a pie-shaped rock that acted as a fulcrum. And he had to do all this while keeping the nine-ton rock suspended in the air!

Solly suggests that Ed created a wooden mold and filled it with cement and placed the shaft into it. When the cement cured, the shaft stood in place and the hole around it was perfect.

For those who doubt that Ed's pulleys and hand tools could have created Coral Castle, Solly's theory of the rocks being filled or put together with some type of binding agent, which Solly calls ancient cement, could be the answer.

Another possibility involving forgotten technology is demonstrated by a retired carpenter in Flint, Michigan, named Wally Wallington, who is currently in the process of erecting his own Stonehenge. Having spent thirty-five years in the construction business, he developed a technique of inserting stones beneath a heavy piece and using them as fulcrums.

Wallington has found that moving and placing giant stones involves finding the stone's center of gravity and understanding basic laws of leverage. He places two round stones approximately nineteen inches apart and uses them as alternating fulcrums. On his Web site, www.theforgottentechnology.com, Wallington explains:

"I found that the heavier an object is the easier it is to balance it. Since mass has to obey the laws of physics, it resists movement and once it is set in motion it resists change. Also, once a weight is close to balance on a single point, rotation can be initiated and the object becomes stable. The more weight, the more inertia, the more inertia, the more stable, therefore the heavier the better. Additional weight or leverage is used and can be shifted so the weight can be balanced on more than one fulcrum. For horizontal movement the fulcrum is also a pivot. Since leverage is not used under the object it does not interfere with motion. In the classes of levers, the lever is always in contact with the fulcrum, input, and the load. When I am using leverage or weight as input, it only comes in contact with the load and the load rests on the fulcrum. Therefore, the load is my lever."[7]

In a recent newspaper article, he adds, "The levers to move the stones of Stonehenge are still there. They are the stones themselves."[8]

Wallington declined to be interviewed for this book, preferring, like Ed, to maintain his privacy. But unlike Ed, Wally has explained his method in detail. He has, in fact, posted a video showing that method in action on his Web site. Videos from other news agencies are posted on You Tube as well. In these videos, Wally is seen pushing around ten-ton cement blocks with ease and even cantilevering them to stand upright. He is not a stonemason and makes no attempt to sculpt the heavy pieces, but watching him work allows us to imagine Ed using similar methods in the creation of Coral Castle.

Other than the alleged, undocumented report about Homestead teens who witnessed Ed levitating the rocks,[9] the notion that Ed had somehow employed supernatural powers to create his castle seems to have begun after his death. Neighbors at the time thought he was a skilled craftsman, a genius, a nut, even a spy, but none publicly bestowed upon him otherworldly connections. Newspaper articles published in the aftermath of his death in the 1950s and '60s, make no mention of such ties.

Except one. The first public conjecture of Ed's involvement with aliens may have been made in 1959 by occultist George Williamson,

George Hunt Williamson (left) was a key figure in the UFO craze during the 1950s.

who wrote and lectured about the existence of UFOs. He and his colleagues published books in the 1950s claiming they had contacted UFOs, usually through the use of a Ouija board.[10]

A small article titled "Coral Castle Holds Secret of Saucers?" in the July 20, 1959, edition of the *Miami Herald* announced that George Williamson, "a noted scientist" would be giving a lecture at Miami's New Age church. The article (which appears without a byline) went on to detail Williamson's claim "that the principles used in creating Coral Castle...might be the same as those which power flying saucers." Williamson also compared the castle to "ancient Inca walls in Peru," noting "both Leedskalnin...and the ancient Incas may have known the secret to the same magnetic force that possibly powers unidentified flying objects."[11]

Whether or not this article sparked visits to the castle—or to

Williamson's lecture—is not known. Speculation about UFOs and about space exploration was quite popular at the time, particularly after Russia launched the earth-orbiting Sputnik space satellite in 1957. Science fiction movies, novels, and magazines captured the country's imagination. The *Herald* article describes "Dr. Williamson" as "an anthropologist who has written several books and is listed as an expert on American Indians by Who's Who. He said he became interested in unidentified flying objects in 1947 when he found the descriptions of sightings were similar to those of many Indian legends."

The article most likely was taken from a press release announcing the lecture and was written by Williamson himself or by someone at the New Age church. In fact, he was neither a doctor nor an anthropologist nor "a noted scientist." To appear in a "Who's Who," one simply must pay for a listing. In his, Williamson apparently bestowed upon himself a doctorate and a background in anthropology. His short academic career actually ended in 1951, when he flunked out of the University of Arizona.

Williamson provided a somewhat dubious beginning to Coral Castle's legacy of supernatural speculation. The theory that aliens were involved in the construction of earthly structures received much more favorable and widespread attention in mainstream media a decade later, through the work of Swiss author Eric von Daniken. In his bestselling books—especially *Chariots of the Gods*, first published in 1968 and made into an award-winning documentary in 1970—von Daniken proposed that some of the earth's ancient mysteries could be accounted for by the presence of "ancient astronauts" from outer space. For example, those astronauts, he suggested, may have taught the Egyptians how to build the pyramids, using alien technologies—much more sophisticated technologies than any culture on earth possessed at the time. The "ancient astronauts" theory received renewed attention through Rod Serling's 1974 television special titled *In Search of Ancient Astronauts*.

When asked how he built his castle, Ed had often offered the cryptic reply: "I know the secrets of the pyramids." Those who share von Daniken's beliefs conclude that Ed, as well, had the benefit of alien technologies to aid his efforts.

Those beliefs are given a certain amount of credence through the pie-shaped stone on which Ed's nine-ton gate balanced for more than forty years. Questions such as where that stone had come from and how such a small rock (approximately twelve inches in diameter and not more than an inch or two thick) was able to balance nine tons without crumbling for over four decades have provided substance for all kinds of theories over the years.

An alleged analysis by the geology department at the University of Florida concluded that the stone was of "unknown origin." Did that conclusion from an esteemed university mean it was not made of a substance found on earth?

We contacted the geology department at the University of Florida to confirm the report of the lab analysis but did not receive a reply. Author Joe Bullard said in our interview with him that he has experienced similar resistance from the school.

Edward Leedskalnin was never a man to do things on a small scale; Coral Castle provides evidence of that. So, too, does the pamphlet he published in 1946: *Magnetic Current.*

The statements he made in its pages were bold and unwavering. The textbooks, Ed declared, were wrong. He had come up with a new way of understanding such significant concepts as gravity, electricity, and magnetism. Though complex—some would say indecipherable—Ed's theories had at their heart a simple premise. He believed that the earth had a magnetic core and that everything on it (animal, vegetable, and mineral) was made up of magnets, each with a North and South pole. The magnetic pull of the earth's core on those poles was responsible for what we know as gravity.

Ed explained: "The North and South pole individual magnets are the cosmic force. They are the building blocks of nature's perpetual transformation of matter, and they are so small that they can pass through everything."[12]

Therefore, to break the law of gravity one merely had to change the polarity of an object.

In looking for explanations of how Ed was able to move around multi-ton blocks of coral with ease, many stop their search here. They believe that Ed, somehow, found a way to reverse the polarity of his huge stones, causing them to float into the air and come to rest precisely where he wanted them. He created, in short, an anti-gravity device.

What did he use as his source of power to reverse that polarity and then sustain it long enough to lift and place the rocks?

The answer to those who favor this theory is obvious—the perpetual motion machine he refers to within the *Magnetic Current* pamphlet. The device he allegedly attempted to receive a patent for; the device, that according to some, drew the attention of Federal officials during the height of WWII.

This "perpetual motion machine" may have been his magnetized flywheel—connected to a reciprocating motor that kept the wheel turning and the magnets polarized. No such motor is displayed in Ed's tool room, though it's possible that it was stolen after Ed's death, when the castle sat vacant for many months. The flywheel today contains no magnets. It is simply a rusted gear with a handle. In a well-known photo, Ed holds the handle and appears to be turning the flywheel. If he needed to continue cranking the wheel to keep it in motion, how did he then use the current it generated to move the stones? Even Ed couldn't be two places at the same time. But if he

Ed cranks the handle on his flywheel, which he called his "perpetual motion machine."

Ed is sometimes compared to another "outlaw" theorist
of electromagnetism, Nikola Tesla.

had discovered a way to keep that flywheel perpetually in motion, he
could have used it to power his system.

Perhaps Ed did intuit a new way of seeing some of the forces that
hold our world together. Perhaps his theories, properly understood,
would advance the understanding of electromagnetic phenomena.
During the 1940s, when he was studying the subject, much work
on it was being done. The ideas of Albert Einstein and Nikola Tesla
sparked exciting new research, opening up possibilities that had previously seemed merely the stuff of fantasy. Anti-gravity was one of
these ideas. Ed may have been swept up in the excitement and begun
expounding and experimenting on his own.

A quick tour of the Internet reveals many who believe that Ed did indeed make significant breakthroughs in electro-magnetic theory. Two researchers at www.leedskalnin.com have even begun attempting to duplicate Ed's experiments in *Magnetic Current*. A number of thought-provoking articles have been written in support of Ed's claims. One of the best is "The Incredible Mystery of Coral Castle," by Christopher Dunn, who concludes, "I have no doubt that Leedskalnin told the truth when he said he knew the secrets of the ancient Egyptians."[13]

Brian Dunning at www. skeptoid.com remains, not surprisingly, skeptical. On his Web site, where he posts a popular podcast, Dunning, a science journalist, states, "I've read [Leedskalnin's] pamphlets on magnetism…and to me they're quite childish." In a personal interview, he added, "[Ed] was using scientific words without any sense of what they mean. He believed that he had great knowledge, but anyone who reads it knows that he doesn't know what he's talking about. It's just gobbledygook. He is asserting that every natural science is wrong, but it's certainly not something that he proved in any way."

When asked if Ed's theories should be more deeply investigated, Dunning responded, "There's no plausible foundation for anything he says. I didn't encounter anything in Ed's books that seems to be worth investigating."[14]

Some would say the same of Ed's other published work—in particular, a booklet he titled *A Book in Every Home*, which, though it contains nothing remotely resembling 'pseudoscience' or the supernatural in its pages, is as controversial among some of the castle's devotees as any of Ed's other writings.

✦ ✦ ✦ ✦ ✦

Ed holds his self-published booklet titled *A Book in Every Home*,
probably sometimes in the late 1930s.

Published in 1936 by the *Homestead Leader-Enterprise*,[15] *A Book in Every Home* is divided into three sections; Ed's Sweet Sixteen, Domestic Life, and Political Life. The text is skimpy, to say the least. Ed fattened the booklet by putting a blank page next to every one he wrote. As he explained: "Reader, if for any reason you do not like the things I say in this little book, I left just as much space as I used so you can write your own opinion opposite it and see if you can do better."

The contents of the booklet invited such commentary. Some of his ideas are disturbing, to say the least. For someone who was always described as shy and sweet natured, Ed revealed a startling rigidity throughout the booklet. His views on love and romance are revealed as surprisingly stern—sometimes even frightening.

He began the pamphlet with an explanation.

"Now I am going to tell you what I mean when I say 'Ed's Sweet Sixteen.' I don't mean a sixteen year old girl, I mean a brand new one."

Ed goes on to explain that he wanted a girl who was pure and sweet, who had never been with another man and never had been in love before. "As soon as a girl acquires experience the sweetness begins to leave her." He, for one, would not have a girl who another man had already "soiled," and he doesn't mean simply that he wanted a virgin. He wanted a girl who had never been in any type of relationship at all.

"A girl is to a fellow the best thing in the world," he writes, "but to have the best one second hand, it is humiliating.... I will put gunny sacks on before I will wear another man's clothes, and this is only a step from having another fellow's girl."

How, though, to keep a young girl "brand new?"

Ed advises mothers to "pose as an experimental station for that fresh boy to practice on and so save the girl."

These views had their genesis in the old country, no doubt. Perhaps they were acceptable there, but in America, where women enjoyed considerably more freedom than rural Latvia, they would have been seen as backward, to say the least. And whether spoken or simply held to himself, they would have made it considerably more difficult for Ed to find a girl he could spend time with, let alone marry.

Writer Agnes Ash, in a February 13, 1966, article in the *Miami News* titled "The Little Man Who Moved Mountains," made that very point.

"...it is safe to suppose that Ed missed the mark as husband material.... He was undoubtedly stubborn, domineering, self-righteous and a painfully unwavering perfectionist. In many ways, Leedskalnin was as unyielding as the coral rock which was his favorite medium of expression."

Ed's views on politics—appearing later in the same booklet—were similarly rigid.

"It is not sound to allow the weaklings to vote. Any one who is too weak to make his own living is not strong enough to vote, because their weak influence weakens the state...."

He continues: "All people are independent so you see everybody will have to take care of themselves and if they cannot, they should perish and the sooner they perish the better it will be."

In the essay titled "Domestic," Ed's ideas come across not so much as frightening as surprisingly mundane. He admits that the first thing he notices about people "is if there is something wrong and if it could be improved." His pointers focus mostly on physical appearance, mostly on the mouth. Ed advises that when one smiles one should be careful to show only teeth, not one's gums. Girls especially should be cautious so that their mouths don't look too big. They should avoid smiling too widely. Mothers should train their children to control how widely they open their mouths, and "children should not be encouraged to smile too much, smiling in due time will produce creases in the sides of their mouths."

Even when taking into account the fact that Ed is not writing in his native language, his ramblings throughout *A Book in Every Home* are so strangely convoluted and pedestrian that some people believe they are coded messages. A man of Ed's genius, these doubters contend, surely must have been able to offer more sophisticated views of life and human nature that the ones printed in this booklet.

✦ ✦ ✦ ✦ ✦

A final group of theorists believe that Ed drew the power he needed to raise the great coral rocks he quarried in Florida City and Homestead from the earth itself. They posit that Ed tapped into what is known as the energy grid, made up of lines—called ley lines—the intersection points of which marked not only Coral Castle's location, but the location point of other megalithic monuments, such as the Dragon's Triangle off the coast of Japan, the megalithic temples of Baalbek in Lebanon, and the Moai heads on Easter Island.

Author Bruce Cathie, as mentioned earlier, believes that Ed's decision to relocate to Homestead was driven by a desire to take advantage of the powers inherent in the grid. Ed, he believes, "knew secrets that some of our scientists would give their right arm for."

New Age occultists share similar beliefs: they claim that the lines denote sources of telluric energy, which is especially powerful at points of intersection.

Those who believe in Ed's connection to von Daniken's ancient astronaut theory link the ley lines to places visited long-ago by extraterrestrials.

All these theories, as mentioned earlier, overlap.

People tend to find in Coral Castle—its existence and its symbols—exactly what they want to find. Those who believe Ed used magnetism will point to the placement of the rocks as proof that they stand on ley lines. Those who believe Ed was somehow linked to the cosmos or was from outer space and somehow using the castle to communicate with extra-terrestrials see in the stars and planets scattered throughout the grounds proof for their beliefs.

Ed's interest in astronomy is obvious as well, though the shapes he used display no unusual knowledge of the subject. One frequently

cited misnomer is his use of the six-pointed star, which many observers have called the "Latvian star." It's not. In fact, there is not
a specific star symbol for Latvia. On some of the country's military
medals, an eight-pointed star is used, but is not known as the "Latvian star" and it does not resemble the stars Ed placed throughout
the castle.

Some countries do make use of a six-pointed star, including the
one above the eagle's head on the Great Seal of the United States.
Some observers have made that connection and see its use as a sign of
Ed's patriotic feelings toward his adopted country.

Ed's six-pointed stars sometimes are seen as Masonic emblems,
proving Ed's involvement with a secret society. Others note the use
of six-pointed stars by the early Egyptians and by the Druids and
thereby conclude that Ed was sending a message about his connection to those groups. Still others see it as a sign of witchcraft.

The star also is interpreted by some to be the Star of David, proving that Ed was Jewish. Some feel it is drawn from Ed's belief in the
old pagan religious customs of Latvia, collectively known as *dievturi*.
Truth is, nearly every religion—from Christian to Muslim to Hindu—
and every culture uses some form of six-pointed star. Ed might have
been referring to any or none of them. Inspiration for the star motif
used throughout the castle might simply have come from the lights he
saw in the night sky while he worked.

As a universal symbol the six-pointed star or hexagram is usually
interpreted to mean the union of the male and female, the yin and
yang. It holds within it the four elements—earth, air, fire, water. Ed
believed in the unity of all things on earth and wrote about magnetic
connectivity. The star could have appealed to him as an expression
of these beliefs, if only on a subconscious level.

Ed also made frequent use of the trilogy motif— the three planets, the three phases of the moon, the three adult chairs in the throne

room, the three bears grotto. This motif is archetypal—it exists in many religions and cultures. To find proof that Ed was drawing from any one religion or culture when using them isn't particularly difficult—or particularly illuminating.

These symbols and others like them are so basic and universal that they can be inserted into virtually any iconographic scheme or theory. Ed put a great deal of thought into his masterpiece, obviously. Given the size and the difficult texture of the pieces, he would have spent weeks or more on a single one, allowing him plenty of time to think about what feelings or meanings he wanted to evoke with it. But his work suggests broad, timeless, universal themes rather than subtle ones. The pieces hark back to his boyhood in Latvia, to celebrations of the natural world, to the changes of season, and the stages of the moon. These themes interested and delighted Ed, and in his amazing sculptures he hoped to delight those who came to see them. Ed's Coral Castle is a monumental piece of folk art, reflecting the joys, sorrows, and obsessions of its creator.

The book *Gardens of Revelation*, by John Beardsley, offers one of the most insightful descriptions of the castle. Beardsley focuses on the castle as a work of art and sees Coral Castle very much as a reflection of the man who created it. He writes:

"The fortress character of Leedskalnin's environment reveals his ideas about independence, self-sufficiency, and the protection of property.... He created a fiefdom in which he could be the undisputed lord. The walls would protect him and his property...from being dirtied by the outside world.... It is...a fantastic horticultural, architectural, and sculptural environment that embodied Leedskalnin's cultural ambitions. And though we may find [his] political and domestic views a little dated, we can take comfort from the fact that he...was innocent of any real power over others. We can celebrate Leedskalnin's work while being relieved that his opinions were forever contained within his walls."[16]

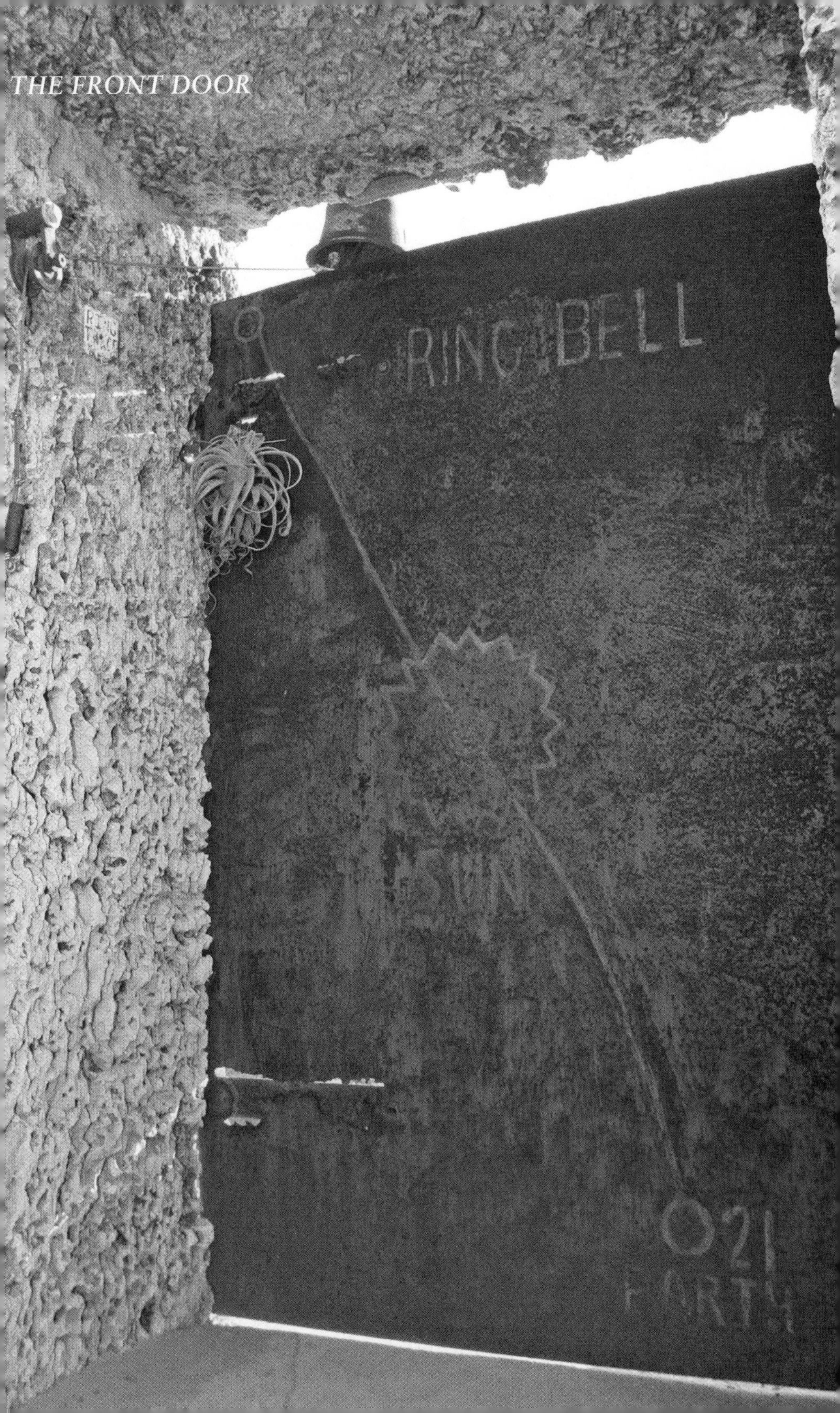

THE FRONT DOOR

THE TELESCOPE

THE TELESCOPE AND 20-TON NORTH WALL

THE MOON FOUNTAIN

RIPLEY'S LARGEST VALENTINE:
THE 5,000-POUND HEART TABLE

THE FLORIDA TABLE COMPLETE
WITH LAKE OKEECHOBEE

THE 40-FOOT, 28-TON OBELISK

THE CARVED, FRESH-WATER WELL

ED'S COOKER CROCK POT

16 STEPS TO ED'S TOWER HOME

ED'S BED, WHICH HANGS FROM CEILING CABLES

THE TOOL ROOM

THE GENERATOR, AKA PERPETUAL MOTION MACHINE

THE THRONE CHAIR

THE SUNDIAL

THE 10-TON GATE

THE CRESCENT

Ed grew up in the shadow of the castles of the German barons that no doubt were embedded deeply in his memory and imagination. His friends, family, and neighbors lived and worked at the whim of these barons, without power and without the ability to significantly change the course of their lives.

When the opportunity arose, Ed built his own castle and became the baron, using the special skills he had developed. He remained an outsider so that inside his castle walls he could remain in control. The walls protected him, just as he protected himself from everyone around him. Everyone who knew Ed recalls that they really didn't know him. He maintained his distance from them.

Within that distance, Ed retained his power. He wrote that scientists did not know what he knew. All the schoolbooks were wrong and lacked his understanding on a variety of subjects. He scorned romantic relationships that did not meet his standards. Stories are told of Ed's fear that the government wanted his knowledge of magnetic currency. They wanted to steal his generator. He would not give it to them. Instead, he died without revealing his knowledge. Even the visitors who paid the admission fee to the castle would hear what he wanted them to hear and when he wanted them to hear it.

For Ed, Coral Castle was above all a place of safety, where a little man with little money could live alone and yet feel powerful. People may disagree on the meaning of his creation or the methods he used to build it, but there is no denying the scope of his achievement. The sheer scale of his creation demanded respect from others. From this respect, Ed drew power. In his own mind, he, too, was large and powerful, and his castle demonstrated that power for all the world to see. A complex man, he imbued his masterpiece with innocence and wonder, with cleverness and romance, building a place that reflected the many sides of its creator.

A view of the Coral Castle courtyard in the 1950s,
when speculation about its supernatural origins began
to catch the country's attention and imagination.

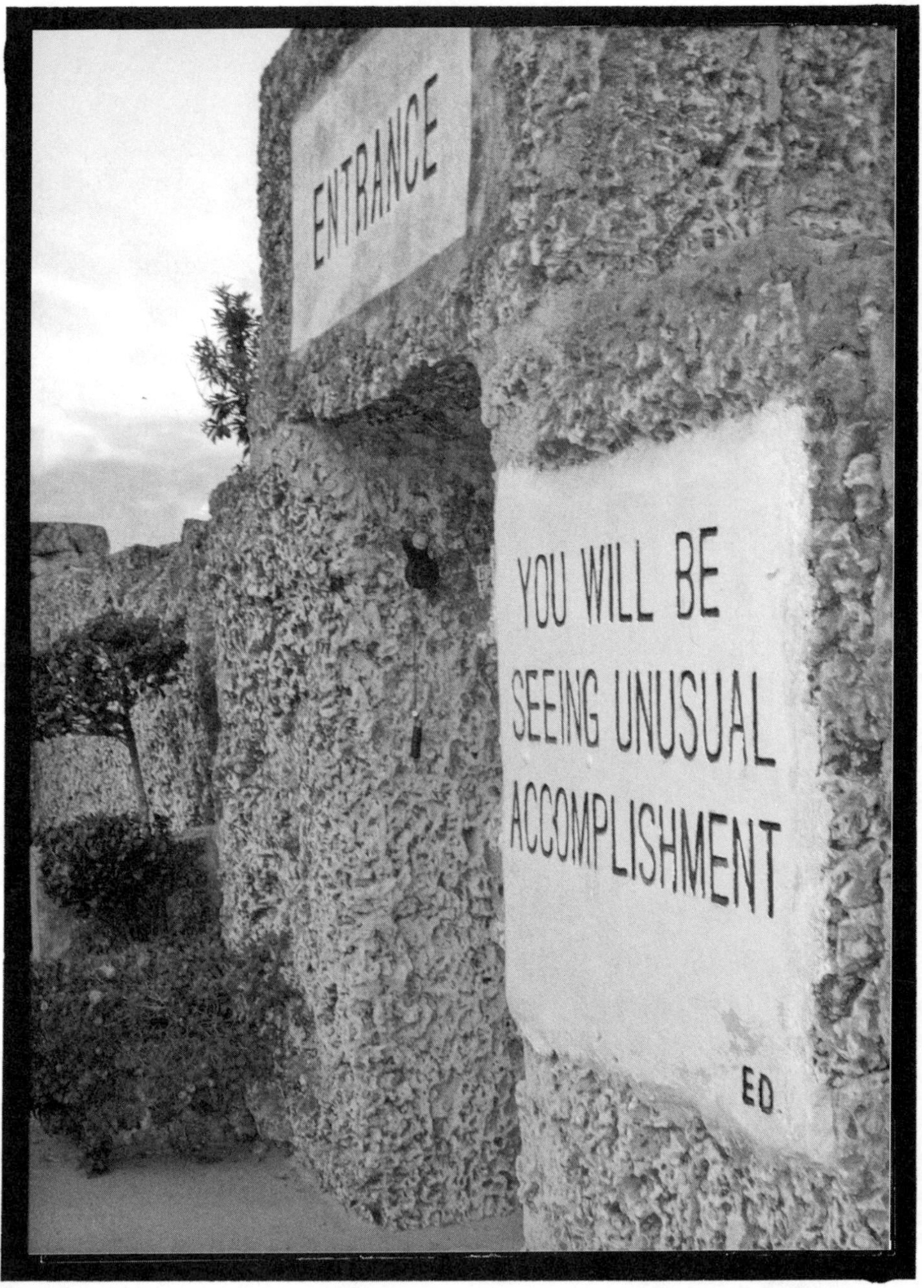
ENTRANCE
YOU WILL BE
SEEING UNUSUAL
ACCOMPLISHMENT
ED

8

A TOUR OF THE CASTLE

Coral Castle is open seven days a week for tourists to visit and admire. Though it remains largely as Ed left it, a tour today is far different from one you would have taken when he was alive.

Ed's castle originally sat on ten acres; the property now has three. Traffic zooms along U.S. 1, the Dixie Highway, not more than thirty feet from the outer wall of the castle. The neighborhood has grown into a busy commercial district of strip malls, gas stations, and chain restaurants. Apartment complexes loom nearby. The typical visitor today first notices the stunning incongruity between the castle's sculpted stone— like some ancient fortress—and the buzz of modern life around it.

The visitor pulls off the bustling highway and parks in a wide, blacktopped lot next to an orange-roofed gift shop and restaurant that also houses the admissions window. Of course, the parking lot and the shop did not exist during Ed's life. To evoke the charm of a tour conducted by Ed himself, the castle now features audio stations, at which a voice claiming to be Ed (in an eastern European accent), offers information as Ed might have given it.

The visitor proceeds up a path, past the trenches from which Ed excavated the rock he used to build the parts of the castle added after the move to Homestead.

In Ed's day a visitor first passed a small sign carved into three-feet-high coral rock that said "ADMISSION 10c. The sign is sculpted to resemble a five-pointed star. That sign still stands outside the castle. Above the stone doorway to the castle, Ed carved the word "ENTRANCE." Next to the doorway he carved a sign to tell visitors "YOU WILL BE SEEING UNUSUAL ACCOMPLISHMENT." Truer words have never been carved in stone.

THREE-TON GATE

The first piece on the tour is the three-ton gate—a flat triangle-shaped stone balanced on a car axle. Despite its enormous weight, it moves easily and looks like a turnstile from *The Flintstones*. Ed had a gift, to say the least, for finding the center of huge stones and balancing them so that they swiveled with the slightest touch. Even after so many decades, the stone still moves freely. And the question still lingers: How was he able to put such a stone in place and balance it on a small axle?

Some believe that the stone directs magnetic energy. A tour guide today will offer to put a visitor to a test to prove the point. The visitor is asked to hold out an arm, and the guide presses down on it, obviously unable to push the arm down. The guide then shifts the angle of the stone and presses again on the visitor's raised arm to show that the arm now drops easily. The experiment is designed to prove the power of harnessed magnetic energy, which some people believe Ed used to lift and place his massive stones. Some visitors are stunned by the exercise; others remain skeptical.

The Three-Ton Gate

ROCK GATE

During his lifetime, Ed called his masterpiece "Rock Gate" or "Rock Gate Park," a name that drew attention to one of the most baffling features of the place. At the rear of the castle stands a nine-ton gate, approximately eighty inches wide by ninety-two inches tall by twenty-one inches thick. This massive stone doesn't simply stand—it's a perfectly hung door, which in Ed's lifetime could be turned with the push of a single finger.

Somehow Ed found the exact center of the rock, bored a hole in the slab and pushed a metal rod through its core. Then he balanced that rod on ball bearings from an old Model T Ford so precisely that the rock gate would spin when pushed by a single finger. The nine-ton stone was set within a quarter-inch clearance of the doorframe by one tiny man. The bearings beneath the shaft rested on a pie-shaped stone that should have crumbled under those nine tons and their rotating torque, the same stone that, decades after Ed's death, the University of Florida geology department analyzed and found to be of "unknown origin."

The gate worked with incredible efficiency until 1986, when its bearings finally rusted out. Resetting the gate required a six-man team of engineers who brought with them a twenty-ton crane and a laser beam. In five days, they finished the job. The gate, however, did not spin as easily as it had in Ed's time.

The engineering team's handiwork did not last. The gate today no longer spins at all.

Did Ed know how to tap into the mythic electromagnetic grid and use some telluric power to set the giant gate? According to an un-attributed article on the Internet, "People who are sensitive to electromagnetic energy fields will sometimes report headaches while standing inside the archway of the nine-ton swinging gate door, thought to be over a vortex and a major grid point of the planet."[1]

THE OBELISK

Near a corner of the castle courtyard stands a twenty-eight-ton, for-ty-foot-tall obelisk, one of the castle's largest pieces and one of the most photographed. The obelisk features a five-pointed star at the top. Sixteen feet taller than the tallest rock structures at Stonehenge, it was the first large piece Ed made when he began building in 1923.

Through the years the obelisk has become symbolic of the castle itself. People often call the star on top a "Latvian star," but research shows that this is not the case. Instead, it suggests Ed's early interest in astronomy, which would become one of the main themes of the castle through planet sculptures and crescent moons and a towering Polaris telescope.

THE WELL

Not far from the nine-ton gate, Ed tapped into the water table and created a well. Again, how he managed to do this—no one knows.

He somehow dug six feet into the ground, much of which was made of coral rock. Locals like to say, "Around here, if you want to plant a tree you need a stick of dynamite." In some places in South Florida, the oolitic limestone runs 4,000 feet deep. It's unlikely Ed used dynamite. Or even a jackhammer. He was able to locate a shal-low spot on his property, perhaps by using a dowsing rod, and drill into it using his primitive tools to create his well.

He then chiseled steps so he could walk down and place jars of food in the cool water for storage. To protect children from falling into the well, he built a low fence around it and carved a round stone that he rolled across the top of the stairway.

Was the well merely a practical necessity built through Ed's ingenious skills, or does it speak to deeper mysteries, ones tied to electromagnetic theories? Some theorize Ed drew more than fresh water from the well; they believe he also drew from it the electromagnetic power that helped him hoist and place his enormous rocks.

THE TOWER

The tower in the southwest corner speaks to the mysteries of Ed's construction method, as well as to the mysteries of the man. Ed lived and worked in the tower, and these areas were not included on the tours when he was alive. His living quarters on the second floor were strictly off limits.

Ed created the tower using blocks that weigh from four to nine tons, set in place and connected with cement. The roof is made of thirty one-ton blocks. In all, the tower weighs 243 tons.

Ed lived on the second floor, accessible by a rock stairway that was carved from a single stone. Much is made of the fact that there are sixteen steps on the stairway, which is seen as yet another homage to his "Sweet Sixteen." Given Ed's obvious attention to detail, it's easy to assume that the number of steps is no coincidence.

The bedroom area is as unique as its inhabitant. The bed is suspended from the ceiling by chains attached to a small pulley, which Ed adjusted according to how high or low he wanted to sleep. He also rigged the system so that he could sleep at various angles. He likely slept at as much as a 45-degree angle to relieve breathing problems that plagued him for much of his adult life—perhaps the tuberculosis that he supposedly cured during his first years in Florida. The ability to hoist the bed to the ceiling also gave him more room in the small area when he wasn't using the bed, which was made from a few boards wrapped in burlap.

More of the tower's mysteries reside on its first floor, where Ed stored his tools and equipment. Guides at the castle have claimed that some of the equipment was stolen soon after Ed died. Pieces that remain are not, at first glance, particularly impressive. The tools he made from old car parts are now coated with rust. It's a motley collection of chisels, blocks, wedges, a couple of pulleys, metal cords, copper wires, and the long steel poles he used to pry up the stones.

RADIO

The tower also contains Ed's radio, which he built from copper wire and Mason jars. He used that radio to keep in touch with the world. Some say that his magna-tricity-amped receiver was powerful enough to grab signals from as far away as his Latvian homeland. Given that he had only a fourth-grade education, Ed must have taught himself the principles of radio during the era when it was still a breakthrough technology. According to reports, he built his crystal set—or perhaps an earlier version of it—as early as the late 1920s, when there was very little programming to be pulled from the sky.

GENERATOR

Near the radio in Ed's tool shop stands what is perhaps the centerpiece of his equipment. It doesn't look all that impressive, just a rusted round flywheel with metal teeth, a metal cloverleaf inside the outer circle of the gear, and a handle for turning the gear.

But Ed's extensive experiments with electromagnetism have sparked belief that the little AC generator was the source of much more than basic electricity for Ed's home. Some people contend that Ed placed magnets on either side of the rotating gear wheel through an ingenious and, to this day, unknown understanding of magnetic fields. These magnets somehow enabled him to bounce electrical current back and forth, creating what amounted to a perpetual motion machine of limitless energy. He refers very clearly and directly to a "perpetual motion machine" in the booklets he published and in advertisements in the Miami newspapers. Somewhat ironically, Ed drew next to no attention after making such a claim. When the man who always kept his work secret finally did come out with a bold public statement he was ignored! Readers probably thought he was crazy to talk about a device that sounded like something from a science fiction novel.

Or maybe they just didn't understand what he was trying to say. When Ed wrote about his experiments with electromagnetism, his lack of a formal education and primitive grasp of written English made his writing difficult to comprehend. Though most formally educated scientists have given his ideas little regard, some theorists do think the generator provided the power Ed needed to lift and place his rocks—and that solving the secret of the generator would solve the secret of how the castle was built.

In the booklet *Magnetic Current*, Ed explains:

"Now about the generator. In the first place all currents are alternating. To get direct currents we have to use a commutator. Transformers and generators of any description are making the currents in the same way by filling the coil's iron core with magnets and letting the iron core push them out and into the coil. Connect the battery with the electric magnet.

"It will be a field magnet now. Put the three-inch coil between the iron prongs and take it out, do it fast, repeat it, then you will have a steady light in the light bulb. Now you and the field magnet are a generator.

"Suppose you had a wheel and many coils around the wheel turning, then you would be making all kinds of light."

Along with "making all kinds of light," of course, there is the suggestion that one could use the power from the generator for other purposes as well...perhaps even to lift rocks weighing thousands of pounds.

THREE READING CHAIRS

Next, the visitor sees three rocking chairs that, despite their weight, still rock with little exertion, a convincing display of Ed's mastery at carving stone. Coral rock has a brittle, pocked surface that is difficult to sculpt into smooth lines, but Ed's shapes still look as crisp as when he made them more than seventy years ago.

Ed placed the chairs at distinct angles so that the sun would be positioned over his shoulder in early morning, at mid-day, and late in the day so he could read. The chairs display an ingenious use of natural light, though it's easy to conclude he also enjoyed the stunt of it—a different chair for various times of day. Ed often posed for pictures in these chairs. Visitors will be surprised to find that the chairs, despite their rough texture, are quite comfortable.

FLORIDA TABLE

One of the most picturesque carvings in the castle, this twenty-foot-long table is shaped like the state of Florida and is surrounded by ten rocking chairs set low to the ground. Ed carved a round bowl into the rock to suggest Lake Okeechobee, which is always visible on state maps. He smoothed cement over the inner surface of the bowl so that it can hold water. (Coral rock is porous and the water otherwise would drain away.)

In talking about this piece, Ed would suggest that someday the governor of Florida might want to use the table to meet with other important political people.

The table, which was made in Florida City and appears prominently in the 1932 advertisement discussed in chapter four, is the only piece with a distinctly local flavor. It seems to have been made expressly for the tourist trade rather than to display his love of science, nature, or his Sweet Sixteen. Those who believe that Ed was not actively seeking interest from tourists even in the early years of the castle have a difficult time explaining the Florida table, which seems to prove that Ed saw the castle as a tourist attraction right from the start.

THE TELESCOPE

Almost as large as the obelisk and perhaps even more impressive, the Polaris telescope, which stands twenty-five-feet high and weighs twenty tons, is located just beyond the castle's outer wall. The telescope is not, strictly speaking, a telescope at all. It contains no reflecting or refracting mirrors and cannot amplify one's view of heavenly bodies. Instead, it functions as a viewing port. It has a carved, round hole at its top with crossed wires, like a gun site, inside the hole. On the inside of one of the castle's outer walls, Ed carved a spy hole with similar crossed wires. Placing one's eye to the hole and centering on the crossed wires in the round hole at the top of the towering telescope, one can see the North Star every night of the year. The North Star moves among the circle's four quadrants as the seasons of the year change.

The telescope and other castle features showcase this modestly educated man's knowledge and fascination with astronomy. It is often mentioned by theorists who claim that Ed's preoccupation with all things celestial suggest Ed was, himself, an alien, or somehow had learned of the advanced technologies brought here during an alien visitation.

THE NORTH WALL

After the telescope, the visitor goes to the North Wall, one of Ed's most enormous pieces. The wall is made up of three stones that stand eight feet high. The center stone weights thirty tons, making it the heaviest part of the castle. Ed topped this stone with two smaller ones placed perpendicular to the wall, a larger stone that runs parallel and acts as the base for a chevron- or gable-shaped stone. The crown, according to Latvian translator Inga Saivena, is a Latvian symbol of the sky. Despite what has been written about the castle's many allusions to Latvia, the North Wall's crown is one of only a few authentically Latvian items in the structure.[2]

And even with this symbol, there is disagreement as to what Ed meant by it. *Waiting for Agnes* author Joe Bullard sees an architectural allusion to the north wall of the King's Chamber in the Great

The North Wall

Pyramid of Khufu, which has a gabled roof that looks like the shape on top of Coral Castle's north wall.

"Ed was saying look at this thirty-ton stone," Bullard explains. "He was telling you that the secret of the pyramids is inside this place. He was saying, 'I understand the secret.' He just saw that configuration of stones and copied it. The beautiful thing about it is that it's in the north wall of the king's chamber. Ed placed it on his North wall. He's just saying that he copied it to show he knows the secret to how these places were built."[3]

MOON FOUNTAIN

In front of the North Wall stands what is called the moon fountain, though it's not truly a fountain, in that no water pours from it. Instead, it is a pool, lined with cement to retain water. The center, circular piece features an undulating interior surface that is amazingly smooth and precise, especially considering the primitive tools Ed used. A six-pointed star graces the middle of the pool, adding yet another symbol from astronomy to the piece.

The Coral Castle tour pamphlet states that "Ed used this part as a fish pond," keeping it full by pumping water from the well. "He usually had fish and hyacinths in the pond and expected visitors to stop and look at his pond."[4] It now functions as a wishing well, glistening with the coins hopeful tourists drop into it.

On two sides of the "full moon" pond rise two large crescents, which symbolize the first-quarter and last-quarter moons. The mix of power and delicacy in the moon fountain make it one of the most beautiful pieces in the castle.

THRONE/THRONE ROOM

The first piece Ed built, back in Florida City, was his chair, which he called his throne. It was an important symbol, one that proclaimed him 'king' of the castle.

The "throne room" itself is made up of a number of chairs, which, like everything in the castle, are made of coral rock. The most prominent chair is Ed's, which in size and weight is surely fit for a king and indicates that Ed truly believed a man's home is his castle—and that the man of the house definitely is in charge. Next to it stands a smaller chair for his Sweet Sixteen, which also indicates his sense of hierarchy—a man should create a place of honor for his woman, but she should remain subordinate to him. Behind Ed's throne stands a smaller chair with a notably rougher texture. Ed created this one for his mother-in-law and hoped that its uncomfortable nature would shorten her visits. No doubt Ed enjoyed the laughter sparked by this little joke. It is one of the few pieces designed for just that purpose.

The "love seat" in the throne room is one of the most unusual pieces in the castle and also one that sheds light on Ed's way of thinking. The love seat features two chairs that face each other, side by side, carved out of a single rock. Ed believed it would be useful when the couple quarreled. Having to face each other, they would talk and resolve their differences and then could kiss and make up.

Perhaps the most widely photographed area of the castle, the throne room is backed by three large planets: Mars, Saturn, and a crescent moon. According to the official tour pamphlet, Ed called the moon figure "the Crescent of the East." These eye-catching shapes have drawn curious visitors to the castle since Ed first created them. Ed allegedly believed that life existed on Mars and to symbolize that conviction he planted a palmetto tree in the stone. Through the years, thousands of people have posed for a photo while curled in the curve of the moon. During Ed's time, and even through the years when the Levin family owned the castle, a visitor could climb a metal ladder on the east wall behind the crescent and slide easily into the piece for a photograph.[5]

SUN COUCH

Near the throne room area, Ed created a flat, circular bed known as the "sun couch." The couch swivels on a brake drum so that Ed could face the sun directly at various times of the day. Joe Bullard and others believe, as stated earlier, that Ed may have used this couch to lie in the sun as a treatment for his tuberculosis, treatment that also included a kind of magnetic therapy. Bullard further says he was told by long-time resident J.T. Bullard that a neighbor saw Ed giving himself this treatment while lying *under* the sun couch.[6]

No proof of such activity exists.

The Sun Couch

SUN DIAL

Ed created his sundial to record the hours between 9AM and 4 PM, which he supposedly said are the times when a man should work—an odd belief for someone who worked through the night. The sundial is accurate enough to determine the time of day within a couple of minutes throughout the year. During Ed's life we did not switch to daylight savings time during spring and summer, and so the sundial remains on standard time. The piece is one of only a few sundials in the world that work in the manner that Ed devised.

BATHROOM AND BEDROOM

Continuing along the eastern wall, the visitor finds Ed's bathroom, complete with a tub lined with cement to retain water. Ed would fill the tub with water from the well and then allow the Florida sun to warm the water for a bath later in the day. Visitors tend to notice the small size of the tub, which does not seem large enough

The Bathtub (above) and the Bedroom (below)

to accommodate a man, but we recall that Ed was a little guy. On the wall above the tub, Ed has carved yet another six-pointed star.

Next to the bathroom, Ed "furnished" a bedroom for his family. He created a bed for himself and one for his wife. He built two smaller beds for their children, along with a crib that rocks.

REPENTANCE CORNER

The most disturbing element of Coral Castle, Repentance Corner provides a somewhat frightening look into the mind of Ed Leedskalnin. In this corner Ed carved two shapes that look like upside-down exclamation points. When a child misbehaved, his or her head would be put through the round opening at the top and locked in with a piece of wood. Ed made a seat for himself and with the child firmly locked into what amounted to a stockade, Ed would lecture them about their transgressions. He also made one for his wife—for when she misbehaved. She, too, would be punished and would be lectured about what she'd done wrong.

Repentance Corner clearly shows that Ed saw himself as lord of the manor and that as such, he was entitled to punish other family members for their shortcomings.

FEAST OF LOVE TABLE

Not far from the family stockade he placed a five-thousand-pound heart-shaped table as a daily sign of his love for his Sweet Sixteen. He carved a hole in the center of the table where he planted an Ixora, which would ensure his wife would have flowers every day. He told his visitors that men are sometimes thoughtless and forgetful and he didn't want to disappoint his wife. Ripley's Believe it Or Not declared the table the largest Valentine in the world.

Repentance Corner

GROTTO OF THE THREE BEARS

This area was designed to be the children's playground. It features three little beds and three little chairs, a stool and a porridge bowl. These pieces all allude to the fairy tale of Goldilocks and the Three Bears. Ed could have known the tale from his own childhood, and it may have been one of his favorites. No record remains of why he chose this tale among all the others. It shows both Ed's childlike nature as well as his love for children. Visitors to the castle while Ed was alive are unanimous in saying Ed was especially kind to children and may have felt more comfortable around them than around adults.

LATVIA

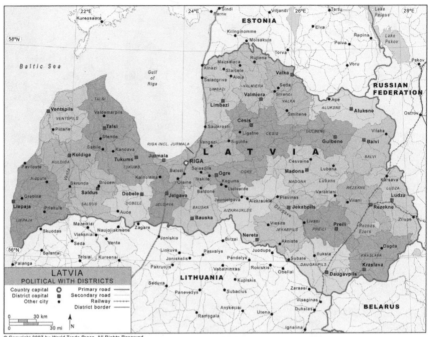

CORAL CASTLE

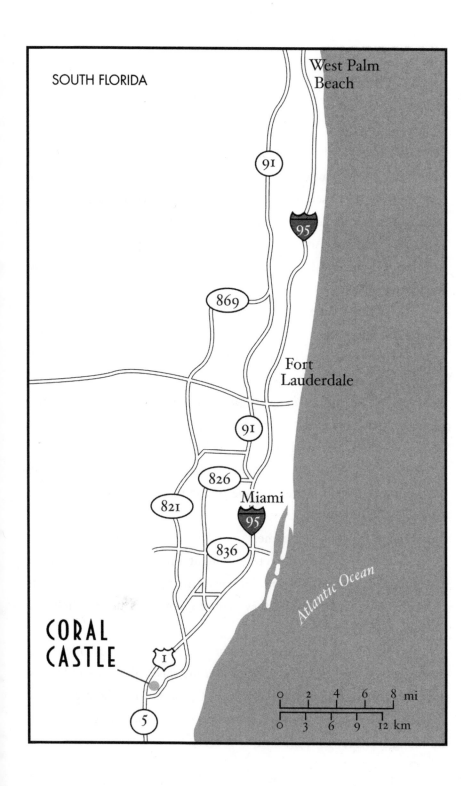

EPILOGUE

Those who publish lists of oddities promote Coral Castle primarily for its place in regional history—a unique remnant of mid-twentieth century roadside kitsch that proliferated along Florida highways. They place Coral Castle next to dancing mermaids, monkey jungles, and glass-bottom boats. Across the American landscape and down Route 66, Coral Castle can be found in directories next to such oddities as CarHenge.

To us, Coral Castle occupies a hybrid position in the greater world. It stands between Stonehenge—because Ed Leedskalnin set megalithic rocks on end—and the Taj Mahal, the three-dimensional wonder-of-the-world-lament to a love lost.

In the classic film *Field of Dreams*, Ray Kinsella follows a whispering voice that tells him, "If you build it, they will come." And so he builds a baseball diamond in his cornfield.

Edward Leedskalnin told many of his visitors that he had built it so that *she* would come...to one of the world's most unusual and mysterious structures.

He built it. She never came.

This Gatsbyesque character's lament might have had F. Scott Fitzgerald revving up his pen. However intriguing the Agnes Scuffs explanation, the bigger mystery remains *how* this underwhelming individual did it.

What lies beneath this saga of lost love might have provided grist for Verne and Clancy, though Ed's *Nautilus* was real, his *Red October* more potent than stealth doors. Coral Castle is so authentic it is on the National Historic Registry; it is so potentially potent it would pull Ed along side Newton, Einstein and Tesla.

That no one really witnessed the one-man engineer working; that he seemingly used only basic technology; that he never explained the meaning of the castle's remarkable design to anyone; that this eccentric scientist took his secrets to his grave; have all provided a mosaic of theories as colorful as the many personalities who are drawn to Homestead, Florida.

How, then, did he do it?

The questions resonate.

We believe there remains more to this castle than meets the eye.

NOTES

CHAPTER 1

1. According to genealogist Sharon Carmack, in a 2009 interview, as a rule of thumb, records signed by or recorded directly by the person being researched are trusted over others. As are earlier records more than subsequent ones. This makes the January date more believable.

2. Interview in 2009 with Dr. Thomas Lorman, professor of Eastern European Studies at the University of Cincinnati

3. Interview in 2009 with Latvian translator Inga Saivare.

4. Lorman interview, 2009. He states the Leidskalnins most likely were Lutheran: "Ninety-nine percent probable, because he's from the east."

5. Sources on the internet—and even at the Coral Castle museum—state that Ed had a fourth-grade education, though we found no documented evidence or even a primary source for this belief.

6. The capsule history of Latvia in the late nineteenth and early twentieth centuries was compiled from a number of sources, but relies most upon: Andris Straumanis, "Latvian Americans." www.everyculture.com; Visvaldis Mangulis, *Latvia in the Wars of the 20th Century*. Princeton Junction: Cognition Books, 1983; Dr. Raimonds Cerūzis, Factsheet published by the Latvian Institute, University of Latvia, 2007-2008.

7. The source of this information is Otto's son Evald, as quoted in *Korallu Pils,* by Andris Stavro. Izdevnieciba 2005, page 43.

8. Andris Straumanis, "Remembering the 1905 Revolution." Published on www.latviansonline.com, January 13, 2005.

9. According to Andris Stavro, author of the Latvian work *Korallu Pils* (Coral Castle),

10. *Korallu Pils,* by Andris Stavro. Izdevnieciba 2005, page 44. Translated for us by Inga Saivare, 2009.

11. Maruta Karlis, *The Latvians in America*, Oceana Publications, 1974, page 6.

12. Stavro, *Korallu Pils,* page 56

13. Interview with Andris Straumanis, 2009

14. Stavro, *Korallu Pils*, page 55.

15. In his article "A Monument to Love: The Coral Castle," which appeared in the 1969 Latvian annual publication *Labietis*, author Arvids Brastins reveals that Ed was in love with a woman named Hermine Lusis, two years his junior, and alleges that Ed proposed to Hermine and, when turned down, asked her to join him in America. Brastins offers no documentation to support his claim.

16. Stavro, *Korallu Pils*, page 56.

17. Lorman

CHAPTER 2

1. (or Worsell)

2. U.S.S. *Pennsylvania* passenger list

3. The age fits his stated birth date of January 12, 1887. Most sources say that Ed was twenty-six, ten years older than Agnes, when he came to America.

4. Charlotte Schmunk interview, 2009.

5. Ruth Campbell interview, 2009.

6. Frances Boysen interview, 2009.

7. Sharon DeBartolo Carmack interview, 2009.

8. Thomas Lorman interview, 2009.

9. Andris Straumanis interview, 2009.

10. Robert Ficken interview, 2009. Dr. Ficken is the author of *The Forested Land: A History of Lumbering in Western Washington* (Washington University Press, 1987) and other books on Northwest history.

11. According to a report by genealogist Sharon DeBartolo Carmack, based on information from *Uncle, We Are Ready: Registering America's Men, 1917–1919*, by John J. Newman (North Salt Lake, Utah: Heritage Quest, 2001):

"Able-bodied men between the ages of eighteen to twenty and thirty-one to forty-five were required to register. At least one in five men who registered in all three drafts were foreign born, with about 3.8 million who were not yet naturalized citizens like Edward. Local draft boards where large numbers of immigrants lived were required to have interpreters on hand, but it is uncertain whether there was anyone who spoke Edward's language in Douglas County, Oregon, or if he spoke enough English by this time."

12. Robert Ficken interview, 2009.

13. William Jinx, "How One Man's Love Turned to Stone." *Miami Herald* Sunday "Tropic" section, May 14, 1972. William Jinx provides a vivid depiction of scenes in Ed's life, but unfortunately he provides no documentation or mention of his sources. Given that some of his scenes rely on details known to be incorrect, we don't put much faith in his assertions about Ed's time in California.

CHAPTER 3

1. www.floridahistory.org
2. Official Web site of Florida City, Florida. www.floridacityfl.gov.
3. Jean Taylor, *The Villages of South Dade*, self-published in 1985. Page 194.
4. Interview with Joe Bullard, 2009.
5. Taylor's description of Ed weighing "ninety-seven" pounds is oddly specific, and that weight appears in a number of descriptions of Ed on the internet. The likely source of such a specific weight is the famous advertisements of Charles Atlas, who promised to turn "ninety-seven-pound weaklings" into musclemen. No documented evidence of Ed actually standing on a scale to be weighed has ever been found.
6. Notarized affidavit signed by E.L. Lawrence, April 24, 1955.
7. April 2005 edition of the American Thoracic Society's American Journal of Respiratory and Critical Care Medicine.
8. Notarized affidavit signed by Florida City resident Mrs. C.U. Barnes, April 24, 1955.
9. Ibid.
10. Taylor, page 194.
11. Coral Castle affidavit collection, Historical Museum of Southern Florida. The affidavits quoted throughout this chapter and throughout the book are taken from this collection
12. Interview with M.C. Bardsley, 2009.
13. Coral Castle affidavit collection, Historical Museum of Southern Florida.
14. Ibid.
15. Ibid. This affidavit, unlike the others, was signed and witnessed in 1994.
16. Carroll Lake, "Projects of Florida Builder Baffle Engineers." *Civil Engineering* magazine. April 1958.
17. Ibid.

CHAPTER 4

1. Edward Leedskalnin, *A Book in Every Home*. Self-published in 1936. Page 1.
2. Interview with Charlotte Schmunck, 2009.
3. In a letter he wrote to his brother Otto in 1950, he says that he hasn't written to anyone in thirty-five years and has forgotten how to write in Latvian. That letter is included in full later in this book.

4. The theories about Hermine Lusis and Lois Moser are presented by Andris Stavro in his book *Korallu Pils*. The author produces no documentation to support either claim.

5. Irwin, page 26

6. Irwin, page 24.

7. Irwin, page 26.

8. Interview with Ruth Campbell, 2009.

9. "Ed Is Doing a Colossal Job of Moving But He Wants No Help, Thank You." No byline. *Redland District News*, July 1939 (exact date unknown).

10. Irwin, page 29.

11. William Jinks, "How One Man's Love Turned to Stone." May 14, 1972, edition of the *Miami Herald*. Sunday "Tropic" section.

12. *The Skeptics Dictionary*.

13. Bruce L. Cathie, *The Energy Grid*. Adventures Unlimited Press, 1997. Page 235.

CHAPTER 5

1. Land deed, Dade County Probate Court records

2. Quit-claim deed, Dade County Probate Court records.

3. Irwin, page 29.

4. Irwin, page 32.

5. Jean Wardlow, "The Lonely Philosopher of Florida's Stone Castle." *Miami Herald* Sunday magazine, April 22, 1962. Pages 5–7.

6. Irwin, page 30.

7. Notarized affidavit signed by Mrs. C.U. Barnes, April 24, 1955.

8. Notarized affidavit signed by Lula Belle Tisdale, April 15, 1955.

9. Notarized affidavit signed by Georgia Neill Waters, April 17, 1955.

10. Notarized affidavit signed by Mrs. Ruth Tomerlin, May 12, 1955.

11. Interview with Frances Boysen, 2009.

12.Irwin, page 20.

13. Ibid.

14. Interview with Ruth Campbell, 2009.

15. Interview with M.C. Bardsley, 2009.

16. Notarized affidavit signed by an indecipherable name on May 9, 1955.

17. Notarized affidavit signed by C.F. Waldron, May 18, 1955.

18. Campbell.

19. The history of Homestead Air Force Base draws primarily from the base's Web site, which is www.homestead.afrc.af.mil.

20. The Freedom of Information Times, www.foitimes.com

21. Irwin, page 52.

22. In our interview with him, Joe Bullard, author of the novel *Waiting for Agnes* and long-time researcher on Coral Castle, stated that rumors existed among the local Homestead folks that Ed had been warned about arrival of the deputy and the government agents.

23. www.code144.com

24. Notarized affidavit signed by Howard B. Johnson on May 23, 1955.

25. Notarized affidavit signed by Herman J. McConnell on April 17, 1955.

26. Interview with John Landgrave, 2009.

27. Notarized affidavit signed by Anne Biggers Couch on April 22, 1955

28. Interview with Frances Boysen, 2009.

29. Andris Stavro, page 167.

30. Ibid.

31. Notarized affidavit signed by Samuel C. Herndon, Sr., April 20, 1955.

32. www.mayoclinic.com

CHAPTER 6

1. Interview with Ruth Campbell, 2009.

2. Karlis, page 31.

3. Stavro, page 201.

4. Dade County Probate Court records.

5. Julius Levin obituary, *Chicago Sun-Times*, April 14, 1990.

6. Interview with Linda Leibsker, daughter of Julius Levin, 2009.

7. Florida's Lost Tourist Attractions (www.lostparks.com).

8. Advertisement for Coral Castle, from the archive at the Historical Museum of South Florida.

9. Ibid.

10. Leibsker.

11. Ibid.

12. "Santo, from King of the Ring to B-Horror Icon—A Biography," by Mike Haberfelner, August 2007, www.searchmytrash.com.

13. Leibsker. The air date of the show come from a mention in a December 1957 edition of the *Coconut Grove Village Post*.

14. International Movie Data Base (www.imdb.com)

15. Interview with Joe Bullard, 2009.

16. In her article "The Little Man Who Moved Mountains," (The *Miami News*, February 13, 1966) reporter Agnes Ash states that Levin "has encountered financial reversals in recent years."

NOTES 159

17. Tim Hollis, *Dixie Before Disney: 100 Years of Roadside Fun*, University Press of Mississippi, 1999. Page 18.

18. "Aladdin City Journal; Animals' Universe Dashed by Wind," by Anthony DePalma. The *New York Times*, 9/22/92. The article focuses mostly on the destruction by Hurricane Andrew of nearby Monkey Jungle and the Parrot Jungle and Garden, which freed many wild animals and birds. DePalma writes, "Someday, if an ambitious and calculating entrepreneur were ever to open a Hurricane World, it would probably include an exhibit on how, with 70,000 homes damaged or destroyed by Andrew, Ed Leedskalnin's castle of coral came through with a scratch and nothing more."

19. Ibid.

CHAPTER 7

1. Frank Joseph, "Mysteries of Coral Castle." *Fate* magazine, July 1998.

2. Interview with Joe Bullard, 2009.

3. www.labyrinthina.com. 1998

4. Jim Solly, "On Proving Ancient Megalith Construction." Copyright by Jim Solly. Reprinted through World-Mysteries.com.

5. Ibid., page 18

6. Ibid., page 19

7. www.theforgottentechnologies.com

8. Charlie LeDuff, "Flint Man Leverages Clever Idea into Monument," *Detroit News*, July 30, 2009.

9. Joseph, op. cit.

10. Alec Hidel, "George Hunt Williamson & the Genesis of the Contactees," *The Excluded Middle* magazine, Number Three. (Undated)

11. "Coral Castle Holds Secret of Saucers?" *Miami Herald*, July 20, 1959.

12. Edward Leedskalnin's advertisement in the *Miami Daily News*, 1946.

13. "The Incredible Mystery of Coral Castle," by Christopher Dunn. Published in *Atlantis Rising*, 1996.

14. Interview with Brian Dunning, 2009

15. According to Orval Irwin, who was working for the newspaper at the time and was told by its editor, Ben Archer, that the paper would be printing the book for Ed.

16. John Beardsley, *Gardens of Revelation: Environments by Visionary Artists*. Abbeville Press, 1995. Page 139.

ACKNOWLEDGMENTS

Writing a book in which much of the story remains a mystery is a daunting task, one we would not have been able to accomplish without the help of a lot of generous people.

Most of all, we want to thank Lissa Kramer, whose research led to many wonderful discoveries and without whom we could not have taken the book to the level we wanted to reach. Thanks, too, goes to Mike Heffron, who researched the pseudo-science and found some great historic photographs.

Genealogists played a key role in our research, mostly through the efforts and patient advice of Sharon DeBartolo Carmack. Her husband, James Warren, also helped with genealogical research, as did Marc Thompson and Teresa Bengal.

Special thanks go to Joe Bullard, author of *Waiting for Agnes*, a fictionalized telling of the Leedskalnin story. He gave us insights and enthusiasm about Ed and the castle. Our appreciation also goes to science writer Brian Dunning, who took time to talk with us and provide his view on the mysteries of the castle.

Dawn Hugh, archives manager at the Historical Museum of Southern Florida, helped immensely with our search for information and photographs, as did John Shipley, the head librarian of the Florida department of the Miami-Dade Public Library. Thanks to both of you.

Our knowledge of Ed's time in Latvia as well as his Latvian heritage was aided immensely by Inga Saivare, who also translated *Korallu Pils* for us. Noted writer and editor Andris Straumanis at www.latviansonline.com answered many questions and offered valuable advice. Latvian-American researcher Amanda Jatniece also helped us understand Ed's world in Latvia.

The world of logging and living in the Pacific Northwest in the early twentieth century was brought to life for us by Dr. Robert Ficken, John Findlay at the Center for the Study of the Pacific Northwest, and Tom Robinson at Historic Photo Archive.

In Homestead and Florida City, we were fortunate to meet many people who offered their memories and ideas. Ruth Campbell at the Pioneer Museum and the Historic Homestead Town Hall Museum was very generous with her time and led us to other local people, such as Vara Hackett and Charlotte Schmunk. Frances Boysen and M.C. Bardsley at the Tropical Everglades Visitors Association took time to share their memories of Ed Leedskalnin, and the center's director, Brian Conesa, generously offered advice and information about people and places in the area.

Bob Jensen at the First National Bank of Homestead supplied great photos, interrupting his vacation to help us. David Peyton, the bank's president, also generously gave us time and advice.

Florida historians Alva Parks and Larry Wiggins gave us important information as well as contact names, helping us understand and evoke the setting for the castle.

At the Coral Castle Museum we want to thank Irene Barr, Sylvia Villafana, and Jon Landgrave for the help with information and photos.

Our thanks to Mike Vraney and Lisa Petrucci at Something Weird Video for the photos and for the quick, gracious response to our request.

In making this book a book, we are grateful to Stephen Sullivan, the cover and interior designer, for his typically outstanding work, to Mark Garvey, editor par excellence, to production and copy editor Donna Poehner, and to intern Adam Riser.

David Stern provided valuable assistance.

The tolerance and love of our families contrasts sharply with Ed's loneliness and we appreciate their being supportive of us.

– Rusty McClure and Jack Heffron

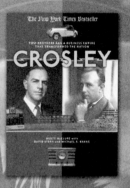

UNIQUE INTERELATIONSHIP LEADS TO THREE GROUNDBREAKING BOOKS

The first book was a national bestseller. The second and third books in a most innovative trilogy are now a reality.

Columbus, Ohio, author entrepreneur Rusty McClure has produced three significant and uniquely related books:

- *Crosley: Two Brothers and a Business Empire that Transformed the Nation*
- *Cincinnatus* (A Novel)
- *Coral Castle: The Mystery of Ed Leedskalnin and His American Stonehenge*

Three related books may never have broken new ground in such a way.

McClure, the grandson of Lewis Crosley, co-wrote *Crosley* with David Stern and Michael Banks. Published in the fall of 2006, the book was the surprise hit of the season, landing on the *New York Times*, the *Wall Street Journal,* and *Business Week* bestseller lists. *Crosley* immediately became the definitive source on a great, untold story in American business history.

McClure and Jack Heffron present another great American story—that of Edward Leedskalnin and his Coral Castle in Homestead, Florida. While several self-published books had been written on the subject, and numerous Websites focus on it, the authors' significant research and serious journalistic approach create their subject's definitive source.

Released simultaneously with *Coral Castle, Cincinnatus* a novel synthesizes elements of both of his nonfiction books. McClure teamed with David Stern to this thriller that draws upon real places and people, including the Crosley brothers and Edward Leedskalnin.

CINCINNATUS

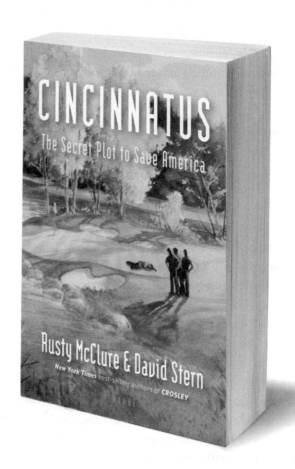

www.cincinnatusbook.com

A compilation of what reviewers have said about Cincinnatus:

Cincinnatus opens with a chapter entitled "1938" introducing Latvian immigrant Edward Leedskalain who has built a "Coral Castle." The chapter serves as a precursor to the rest of the book's mysterious situations and characters.

Rusty McClure and David Stern spin the tale of golf caddy Matt Thurman and a host of government investigators, from the Department of Justice to the Federal Bureau of Investigation. Stretching across the country from Florida to California to Ohio, Cincinnatus is an intriguing foray into the lengths people will go to fulfill an ideal, and how differently that ideal can be interpreted. The characters rarely break from the action and the tension this builds makes the book hard to put down.

What Matt and the Department of Justice's Espy discover is a major plot that evidently has its roots in the "Society of the Cincinnati." Once again, this is a real organization although their involvement in the story here is purely fictional.

From the opening words to the very end the action is virtually nonstop. McClure and Stern have written a novel that is full of intrigue that is made all the more realistic by the inclusion of a real organization, an actual scientific mystery and people who actually lived.

Perhaps the strongest element of the book, however, is the strong character development of not only the major characters but many of the minor characters as well. For much of the book, characters that we grow to trust turn out to be the "bad guys."

With two non-fiction books previously published on topics referenced in this novel, it is clear these two have done their research.

Cincinnatus is a gem and it is nice to have a historical thriller that hits deep in America's roots, and all too believable given the political atmosphere in the United States and much of the world.

Excerpt from *Cincinnatus*

LA GUARDIA was on the radio.

A recorded broadcast, a speech he'd given a week earlier. Scratchy and barely audible over the wind rushing by.

"...we have to quarantine...the germs of Fascism, of Nazism..."

The man at the wheel of the car fiddled with the tuner to no effect. He turned up the volume.

"...there is nothing a democracy can or wants to learn from a dictatorship in Europe. There is nothing that these countries can give any of our countries. There is—"

A burst of static cut off the mayor's voice. The man fiddled again and gave up.

He was driving a dark green 1938 Buick Sport Coupe, heading south on Biscayne Boulevard, the tan canvas top down, the sun shining on his arms, the ocean breeze blowing back his hair. Miami lay behind him, Key West ahead, his destination somewhere in between.

The man's name was Lewis Crosley. He had the build of a football player turned workingman, the hands of the farmer and dam engineer he'd once been. He wore a businessman's suit now, a summer-weight gray suit that felt sticky against his skin.

He wore the suit because at the morning meeting he represented the Crosley Corporation. The afternoon meeting toward which he drove was personal. He had mixed feelings about it, suspecting it was a fool's errand but hoping, for his brother's sake, that he was wrong.

Biscayne Boulevard became Route 1. Four lanes narrowed to two as the road curved inland. Bugs splattered on the windshield. Lewis turned on the wipers, but the bugs kept coming. He kept driving, turned his mind away from his brother's troubles to La Guardia's speech about the Nazis and the approaching war. Any fool could see it was coming. Anyone who thought the trouble in Europe wasn't America's business was kidding themselves. Europe today. America tomorrow.

Bullets. Tanks. Bombs. War.

Good versus evil. It was that simple.

Lewis had done his part, enlisting in the Great War at twenty-seven despite having a wife and young daughter. He'd gone overseas, taken fire in the Argonne. Serve your country, serve the cause of freedom. It was an obligation, like Thomas Jefferson had said. Eternal vigilance, that was freedom's price, one the founding fathers had gladly paid. Lewis's great-grandfather had paid it with them, in 1776. Two of his uncles had paid it in the War Between the States. Each generation had to pay it anew.

He was so busy thinking about America's obligations to the free world he almost missed his destination. He noticed, just in time, a red house on his left, not much more than a shack, which was one of the landmarks Benny had mentioned. "The guy don't make it easy to find, I'll tell you that much," Benny had said as he gave Lewis directions and the keys to the Buick. True enough. The next landmark was a Key West highway sign a few hundred feet past the red house, same side of the road, and Lewis almost missed that one too, buried as it was in the scrub that passed for forest in this part of Florida.

Then Lewis looked to his right, and saw, coming into view...

Edward Leedskalnin's home.

Huge coral stones standing on end, placed together to form what looked like a castle or fortress—stones as heavy as ten tons, as tall as twenty feet, according to the newspaper article, which had called Leedskalnin an eccentric. Benny had said he was a real character. Lewis was beginning to agree. And he was beginning to think Powel, his brother, was going to be terribly disappointed.

Lewis pulled off the road. As he set the parking brake and opened his door, he glanced across the street, which was when he saw the other car—a black Ford Coupe, parked along the shoulder of the highway, up on the dirt, in a little canopy made by the low-hanging Florida scrub. Two men sat inside, staring at him.

The driver wore a dark suit and a Fedora. The man in the passenger seat wore a shirt and tie, no jacket, no hat. The Ford was twenty feet away, close enough for him to see their faces.

They stared so long Lewis felt compelled to speak.

"Morning," he called out.

The driver started the car, and the Ford sped away.

Before Lewis could think about the strangeness of the encounter, he heard a new sound. Someone was coming.

He raised a hand to shield his eyes and squinted into the sun.

The someone, wearing a white shirt and dark pants, was coming on a bicycle, wobbling down a dirt path next to the road. He was still a hundred yards away, passing by a vegetable garden. He sat erect in his seat, looking straight ahead.

He sees me. He's wondering who I am, what I'm doing here.

Which Lewis, not for the first time that morning, wondered himself.

He drained the last of his soda and waited. He normally didn't drink soda, but while driving from Miami with the sun on his neck, the heat roiling from the leather seats, he found himself craving one. When he stopped to ask directions, he'd picked up a bottle of Double Cola. Jacksonville D.C. Bottling Company. Your Local Flavor, Your Local Favorite.

Lewis looked from the soda bottle to a sign announcing "NO TOURS TODAY," then turned to watch the man on the bike, who he felt sure was Edward Leedskalnin.

The man stopped ten feet shy of Lewis and climbed off the bike. He was, as the article had promised, all of five feet tall. And skinny. Wiry-looking though—muscular, not frail. But even if he was all muscle, he couldn't have weighed much more than a hundred ten pounds.

Smaller, Lewis realized, than his wife, Lucy, whose voice he now heard in his head once again: *Fool's errand.*

Lewis stepped forward to greet Leedskalnin.

Which was when he saw the bicycle's tires. They were metal. Bent in spots, accounting for the wobbliness. Who, in this day and age, rode a bike with metal tires?

"Good afternoon," Lewis said. "I hope you don't mind—"

"No tours today, I am sorry. You see sign?" The little man spoke in a high-pitched voice and a heavy European accent, something close to German, with long, sibilant ës's and rolled ër's that made ësorry' come out sounding almost like ësoddy.'

He had dark, thinning hair, combed back from his forehead, bright, piercingly blue eyes set in a rectangle of a face with prominent cheekbones, a prominent jaw, and what looked to be permanent frown lines at the corners of his mouth.

Not a man who did a lot of smiling.

"I'm not looking for a tour," Lewis said. "I was hoping to ask you a few questions—Mr. Leedskalnin, isn't it?"

Leedskalnin grabbed the books from the wire basket on the front of the bike—three thick volumes with brown cloth bindings, paper flaking at the edges.

"Yes. I am Edward Leedskalnin." He pronounced the ëw' in Edward like a ëv': *Edvard.* The ënin' at the end of his last name with a ëy': *nyin.* Edvard Leedskalnyin. "But I am busy today, I am sorry. Come back tomorrow. I give tour. Excuse me."

"But—"

Leedskalnin headed for the building beyond. The soles of his shoes clanged against the rock path as he went. They were metal too.

Lewis watched the little man walk to the front door of his home, which looked even stranger up close than it looked from the road. An eight-foot rock wall surrounded the place. A two-story tower at one corner looked down on the vegetable garden outside the wall and the field and scrub beyond. The place looked like a miniature version of a European castle, one that had been picked up whole out of the French countryside and dropped in the middle of tropical Florida.

A castle, forty-five minutes south of Miami.

Lewis had a hard time believing it. And he wanted nothing more than to turn his back on his brother's errand, on the odd collection of stones lying in the yard and the little man who'd gathered them.

He had a bad feeling. A feeling like none of this was going to come to any good.

Lewis walked past Leedskalnin's garden and was tempted to grab a tomato off the vine. They looked good. Leedskalnin was walking back from the castle, heading straight toward him. Waving a finger.

"What are you doing?" he called out.

"You have mildew," Lewis announced.

Leedskalnin frowned. "I have what?"

"Powdery mildew. On your collards. See?" Lewis plucked a leaf and showed it to Leedskalnin.

"Ah," Leedskalnin nodded. "I have this last year too. All my greens—ruined." The last word sounded like ëruint.'

"You might try spacing the plants out a little more. Let them get a little more sun. Don't water quite as much."

"You are farmer?"

"Long time ago I was. Now I just keep a garden. Start my day out there, five-thirty in the morning. Get my hands in the soil, get the blood flowing...."

Leedskalnin nodded and smiled.

Lewis smiled too. "These days I work in an office. In Cincinnati. With my brother. Which is what I want to talk to you about." He brushed his hands together to clear off the dust. "My name's Crosley, by the way. Lewis Crosley."

When they shook hands, Lewis was surprised at the strength in the smaller man's grip—like a pair of pliers. Rough, callused hands.

"I am please-ed to meet you, Mr. Cross-ley. I will give you tour now. To show my thanks."

"I really just want to talk to you."

But Leedskalnin hurried ahead to the main gate and then to the metal door, pushing it open. Stepped inside and waited for Lewis to follow.

After touring the castle, they talked about the history of Crosley Radio. Crosley Broadcasting. They talked about the technology and about the people and even about the politics. As they talked, Lewis realized the man was starved for conversation. When Lewis mentioned Powel, Leedskalnin's face lit up.

"Ah. The famous Powel Crosley," he said.

Lewis nodded. Powel was as well known as any industrialist in the country. Not just his name, but his face, had come to be associated with everything the company did—the Shelvador refrigerator, Crosley radios, WLW broadcasting, the Cincinnati Reds, and the soon-to-be Crosley Car.

But Lewis saw a side of his brother that no one else got to see. The family man. The loving husband.

"It's because of Powel I'm here," Lewis said. "He needs your help."

"What could I do for your brother that he could not hire ten other men to do?"

"Not for him. For his wife. Her name is Gwendolyn. They've been married almost thirty years. Childhood sweethearts, you could say."

Leedskalnin's expression changed, from puzzlement to something else, a flash of anger, another of sadness, of melancholy.

Man Builds Coral Castle for Lost Love

"She has tuberculosis," Lewis said. "She's very sick. The doctors won't come right out and say it, but it's clear she's dying."

Leedskalnin was silent a moment, perhaps making the connection between Powel's wife and his own lost love. "I'm very sorry to hear this," he said. "Sorry for your brother and his wife. It is a terrible disease."

"You had it, as I understand. A terminal case, the papers said. The doctors told you to go home and get your affairs in order."

"Correct."

"You were supposed to die. But you didn't. You lived. Cured yourself. A miracle cure, they said."

Leedskalnin said nothing.

"So that's why I'm here," Lewis went on. "To find out how you did it."

Leedskalnin remained silent. Lost in thought.

"In the paper they mentioned something about magnets," Lewis said.

"Magnetic therapy." Leedskalnin nodded. "That is what I told the reporters, yes."

Told the reporters. Lewis's heart sank. "So that wasn't true?"

The ghost of a smile flitted across Leedskalnin's face. "Oh it's true. As far as it goes. But not the whole truth."

"I don't understand."

"Do you really want to?" Leedskalnin asked with a spark in his eyes. "They called it a miracle, Mr. Crosley, but it's no miracle. There is nothing supernatural about what I did. In the hospital or what I did here."

"What you did here?"

"How I moved the stones," Leedskalnin said. "How I took this obelisk whole, from the ground, and raised it to where you see it now.

How I rid my body of the illness—the energies invading it. All the same. It's about recognizing the forces around us. Seeing them for what they truly are and learning how to manipulate them."

Lewis tried to mask his disbelief but knew it showed on his face. The little man wasn't just eccentric. He was crazy.

Leedskalnin said, "I can prove to you the truth of what I am saying. I can demonstrate my knowledge of these things in a way that will make you reconsider everything you know."

ABOUT THE AUTHORS

RUSTY McCLURE is the *New York Times* best-selling author of *Crosley: Two Brothers and a Business Empire that Transformed the Nation.* He has a Master of Divinity degree from Emory University and a Harvard MBA. An advisor and investor in numerous entrepreneurial projects, Rusty teaches an entrepreneurial course at his undergraduate alma mater Ohio Wesleyan University. He is the son of Ellen Crosley McClure, daughter of Lewis Crosley. She is the sole surviving direct descendant of the Crosley brothers. He resides with his wife and daughters in Dublin, Ohio.

Rusty is also the co-author, with his *Crosley* co-author David Stern, of the novel *Cincinnatus* which features several non-fiction plot elements. Three of which are Edward Leedskalnin, his Coral Castle and the mystery that surrounds the methodology Leedskalnin deployed.

JACK HEFFRON has written several books of instruction for writers, as well as numerous articles for magazines, primarily on travel, sports, and popular culture.

His work has been noted in Best American Travel Writing and has won awards from the Society of Professional Journalists and Authors.

His column in Cincinnati magazine was recently chosen as the best in Ohio by the Cleveland Press Club. His short stories have appeared in many literary magazines and twice have been nominated for the Pushcart Prize.

He has taught at writers' conferences throughout the country and lives in Cincinnati, Ohio.